Microsoft® Excel®
VBA Guidebook

Second Edition

Allen L. Wyatt

Microsoft® Excel® VBA Guidebook, Second Edition

Published by:

Sharon Parq Associates, Inc.
PO Box 794
Orem, UT 84059

For information on purchasing, distributing, or reselling books published by Sharon Parq Associates, Inc., please visit our website (www.SharonParq.com) or call 801-607-2035. Our books are also available through select online resellers such as Amazon.

ISBN: 978-1-61359-224-3 (printed book)
ISBN: 978-1-61359-225-0 (e-book)
ISBN: 978-1-61359-226-7 (e-book on CD-ROM)

Produced and published in the United States of America

Revision history:

7 December 2011: First published
9 December 2013: Second edition

Content Overview

About the Author

Allen Wyatt, an internationally recognized expert in small computer systems, has been working in the computer and publishing industries for more than three decades. He has written more than 50 books explaining many different facets of working with computers, as well as numerous magazine articles. His books have covered topics ranging from working with programming languages to using application software to using operating systems. Through the written word, Allen has helped millions of readers learn how to better use computers.

Besides writing books, Allen has helped educate thousands of individuals through seminars and lectures about computers. He has presented complex topics to audiences throughout the United States as well as throughout Mexico and Costa Rica. His books, which often form the basis of his presentations, have been translated into many languages, including Chinese, Dutch, French, German, Greek, Italian, Japanese, Korean, Polish, Russian, and Spanish.

Allen is the president of Sharon Parq Associates, Inc., a computer and publishing services company located in Orem, Utah. Besides writing books and technical materials, he publishes a series of online newsletters and oversees the development of the Tips.Net family of websites (www.tips.net).

Allen Wyatt
Sharon Parq Associates, Inc.
PO Box 794
Orem, UT 84059

http://www.allenwyatt.com
allen@sharonparq.com

Detailed Table of Contents

Introduction

Excel provides quite a few features and native capabilities that allow you to slice and dice your data in any number of ways. For many people, these capabilities provide everything they need to have done. For other people, however, these capabilities are just the beginning.

You see, Excel allows you to extend what can be done with the program through the development of macros. (This is why some people refer to Excel as an ***extensible program***—its capabilities can be extended beyond what Microsoft provides.) You create macros using the VBA (Visual Basic for Applications) language within Excel.

That's what this book is about—using VBA to create macros that can extend your use of Exceel. I wrote ***Microsoft Excel VBA Guidebook*** (and subsequently updated it to this second edition) because I could not find a good entry-level guide anywhere for people wanting to learn how to program Excel macros.

Some people are a bit skittish when it comes to macros. They get the same feeling that they get when they go into unfamiliar territory or venture into some new experience. It is easy to feel that way, but there really is no need—macros can be as simple or as challenging as you want them to be. You can work through this book at your own pace, trying out the pieces and parts of VBA that interest you and that make your use of Excel better than before.

Who this Book is For

Every book is written with assumptions about you, the reader. This book is no different; in writing it I tried to make as few assumptions as possible.

First, I assume that you are naturally inquisitive—that you like to "poke around" under the hood, so to speak. When working with a program—and Excel is no exception—I enjoy seeing what this command does or that feature accomplishes. I'm hoping that you are the same way. The "adventuresome spirit" is helpful in learning, particularly in learning a topic as expansive as macro programming.

I also assume that you know a good deal about how to use Excel. Before delving into macros, it is a good idea to have more than a passing familiarity with the major parts of the program. You don't need to know how to use every worksheet function that Excel provides (there are a ton of them!), but you should know what worksheet functions are and how to put together a formula. You should also know basic things, such as how to open, edit, and save workbooks.

It's a plus if you can figure out how to create custom formats and know the basics of conditional formatting. Perhaps you've even ventured into using data validation and creating PivotTables. In short, you should already know your way around Excel, from a user's perspective, before you seek to extend the program through macros.

Another assumption is that you are using one of the latest versions of Excel: 2007, 2010, or 2013. This book was written with you in mind. While VBA has been around since Excel 97, the interface and features of the program were greatly changed starting with Excel 2007. All of the examples and screen shots provided in this book were created and grabbed with these versions in mind. (Virtually all of the screen shots were taken in Excel 2013 running on a Windows 8 system. A few shots specific to other versions of Excel were grabbed on differing systems.)

Finally, I assume that you aren't afraid to try things. You'll get plenty of opportunity to try things out as you work through this book.

What this Book Covers

It is safe to say that this book covers a lot. I've tried to cover everything you'll need to know to start programming your own macros and editing the macros you may get from others. That means I've included everything I consider to be basic and elemental in nature, but I don't just stop there—I also include quite a bit that you will find challenging as you expand your understanding.

If you are brand new to macros (you've never worked in the Visual Basic Editor before), then you'll want to make sure you read the first three chapters in order. They are foundational to everything else you may learn about macros. This is particularly true about Chapter 2, *Elements of Macros,* which covers a ton of ground about VBA in the Excel environment. (You'll definitely want to return to and refer to that chapter over and over again.)

The rest of the chapters in the book cover well-defined topics that expand the basic information you pick up in the first three chapters. You can, if you desire, read them in any order you want, as your programming needs pull you this way or that way. Of particular interest to those wishing to process worksheets and workbooks with macros will be 10 through 13 which focus on using Excel's object model. (The object model is key to understanding how you access different parts of your worksheets and workbooks in Excel.)

As I started updating *Microsoft Excel VBA Guidebook* for the second edition, I paid particular attention to correcting typos and errors that crept into the first edition. (Yes, despite my best efforts there were some errors. Unfortunately there may be some in this edition, as well.) I also fully updated all the screen shots to verify that everything worked with Excel 2013, and I added several new sections about topics as diverse as changing VBA project library references and working with named ranges.

And, as a big plus to this new edition, I added a resources chapter (see Chapter 17). It is provided to give you ideas on next-level VBA programming books that you may find helpful. Each suggested book includes complete information (such as title and ISBN) and a QR code you can use to jump directly to the book's page at Amazon.

What is Not Covered

The topic of macros is so expansive that it is impossible for a single book to cover everything related to the topic. This is especially true when it comes to how Excel is dealt with in VBA. There are a few things that this book does not cover and it is good for you to know, up front, what those items are. Each of these items has been excluded because, quite honestly, they are a bit "out of focus" for an introductory book on Excel macros.

First, this book doesn't cover how you work with some of the more advanced features of Excel. Chief among these are charts and PivotTables. These two items (and a couple of other advanced features) are really deserving of their own book. However, the basics of working with macros—which you can master with the information in this book—apply equally well to working with advanced objects such as charts and PivotTables.

A few other advanced or esoteric topics I don't get into are creating digital signatures for your macros and how to create your own add-ins. I also don't really get into the XML structure of Excel's workbooks and how you can use XML to modify the user interface. All of those are topics better left to treatment in other books.

Finally, I don't really cover how to create custom user forms (custom dialog boxes). VBA has a rich ability to create them, but they seemed—at least to me—to be beyond the needs of who I envision as the average reader of this book. If you want to learn about them, consider a good programmer's reference for Visual Basic; it shares the same capabilities as VBA.

Where to Go Next

If you need more information about programming macros in Excel, I strongly suggest that you consider *ExcelTips: The Macros*. This e-book, currently in its seventh edition, contains hundreds of tips, tricks, and ideas on how you can use macros in ways you may never have thought of. It is a great companion to *Microsoft Excel VBA Guidebook,* providing the "next step" in programming prowess you want.

If you decide you want your own copy of this great book, you can find it here:

`http://store.tips.net`

For a large number of other suggestions on your next programming steps, make sure you refer to Chapter 17 for guidance.

A Word about ExcelTips

I've been using Excel, literally, for decades. I have worked in corporations and used Excel to produce reports and worksheets that helped accomplish the goals of those companies. In 1998 I started a weekly newsletter devoted to tips and ideas on how to use the program better.

That weekly newsletter, *ExcelTips,* is still running strong. It is published every Saturday morning, and you can subscribe for free. More information (including thousands and thousands of online tips) is available at the *ExcelTips* website:

`http://excelribbon.tips.net`

1

Introducing Macros in Excel

When you start to understand the word "macro," you begin to see that it is a word with a rich history, but also one that doesn't always have a good reputation—at least in the programming community. You see, macros are often viewed as nothing more than a series of memorized steps to be performed over and over again.

While Microsoft built into Excel the ability to record a series of steps so you can perform them again and again, macros in Excel are much more than the pejorative term that "real" programmers often envision. In this chapter you'll start to see why this is the case as you create your first macros. Specifically, you'll discover the following:

- Why Microsoft chose VBA as its macro language
- How to configure your system to allow macros
- The two major ways of creating macros
- How to run, edit, and delete macros

Understanding VBA

In the early days of Excel, the program used a macro language that was based upon a scripting language, similar to the scripting languages in other, earlier spreadsheet programs such as Multiplan and Lotus 1-2-3. This was great, as it allowed users to perform common tasks easily and effectively.

Everything changed, however, when Microsoft released Office 97. Ever since then, all the programs in the Office suite (including Excel) have used Visual Basic for Applications (VBA) as their macro programming language. This language is much more powerful than the earlier scripting languages ever could be. It is based upon the popular BASIC programming language, but VBA is essentially a subset of Microsoft's Visual Basic object-oriented programming language.

Because VBA is standardized across all of Microsoft's Office applications, this means that you can learn VBA for one application (such as Excel) and have a great head-start on using the language in other applications (such as Word). It is interesting to note that VBA has been so successful and proved so useful that some other companies, besides Microsoft, have adopted it as the macro programming language for their applications.

Introducing the Visual Basic Editor

When you work with VBA programs, you do so in what is termed the *Visual Basic Editor*. This is a special place in which macros can be worked with in Excel. (You don't work with macros in a spreadsheet; you must work with them in the Visual Basic Editor.) You'll find a full discussion of the Visual Basic Editor in Chapter 4, but it's good for you to have a brief introduction right now, simply because the moment you start using macros you'll run into the Visual Basic Editor.

For now, simply display the Visual Basic Editor by pressing Alt+F11. Your worksheet stays on the screen, but a whole new screen appears. This is the editor, as shown in Figure 1-1.

Displaying the Developer Tab

Ever since the release of Excel 2007, the program has used what is generally known as the "ribbon interface." This simply means that the older-style menus were replaced with a series of tabs, at the top of the screen, that allow you to access Excel's most commonly used features.

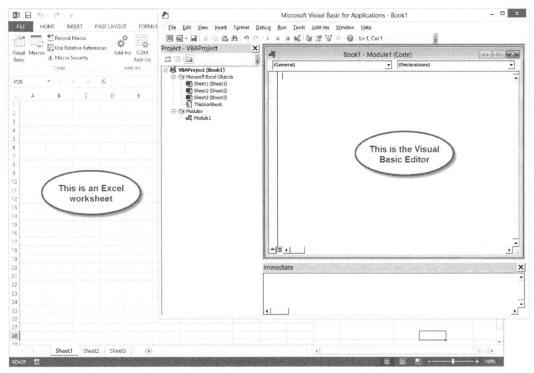

Figure 1-1. *The Visual Basic Editor is where you do your work with macros.*

For those working with macros, one tab that is most helpful to display is the Developer tab. This tab should be visible near the right side of the ribbon.

If you cannot see the Developer tab on the ribbon, then you need to turn it on so that it is displayed. How you turn on the Developer tab depends on the version of Excel you are using. If you are using Excel 2007, follow these steps:

1. Click the Office button and then click Excel Options. Excel displays the Excel Options dialog box.

2. Make sure the Popular option is selected at the left of the dialog box.

3. Ensure there is a check mark in the Show Developer Tab in Ribbon check box (see Figure 1-2).

4. Click OK.

If you are using Excel 2010 or Excel 2013 then the steps are quite a bit different:

1. Click the File tab of the ribbon.

2. Click Options. Excel displays the Excel Options dialog box.

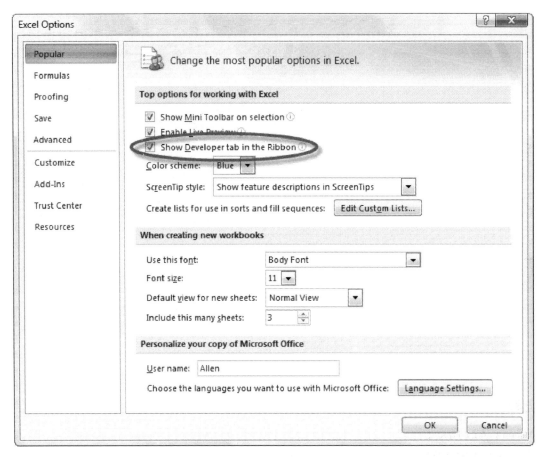

Figure 1-2. *You turn control the display of the Developer tab of the ribbon by using the Excel Options dialog box.*

3. At the left side of the dialog box choose Customize Ribbon.

4. At the right side of the dialog box, make sure the check box at the left of the Developer tab entry is selected, as shown in Figure 1-3.

5. Click OK.

With the Developer tab displayed on the ribbon, you are almost ready to jump into the deep end of the pool and start creating macros. First, though, you should make sure that macros are actually enabled on your system.

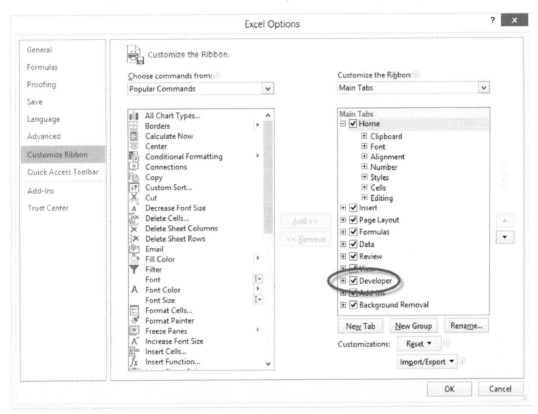

Figure 1-3. In Excel 2010 and 2013 you can control whether any of the tabs are displayed on the ribbon, including the Developer tab.

How to Enable Macros

When you first use Excel, or if you use it for a while without ever having used macros, the program is configured to automatically disable macros. In order for you to start working with macros, it is a good idea to enable them on your system.

There are two ways you can display the Trust Center. If you have the Developer tab of the ribbon available (as described in the previous section), simply click the Macro Security tool in the Code group.

The second way to display the Trust Center involves following these steps:

1. Display the Excel Options dialog box. (In Excel 2007 click the Office button and then click Excel Options. In Excel 2010 and Excel 2013 display the File tab of the ribbon and click Options.)

2. Click Trust Center at the left of the dialog box.

3. Click Trust Center Settings.

4. Make sure Macro Settings is selected at the left of the dialog box.

Once the Trust Center is displayed (as shown in Figure 1-4) you can select a security setting that allows you to run your macros.

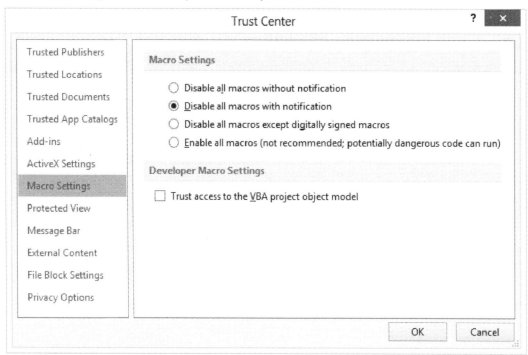

Figure 1-4. The Trust Center is where you specify how Excel treats your macros.

The Trust Center has four settings for macro security:

- **Disable all macros without notification.** All macros and security alerts about macros are automatically disabled.

- **Disable all macros with notification.** Macros are disabled, but a security alert is displayed to allow you to enable macros on a case-by-case basis.

- **Disable all macros except digitally signed macros.** Non-signed macros are disabled, but a security alert is displayed to allow their enabling. If the macro is digitally signed and from a publisher you trust, it is automatically enabled.

- **Enable all macros.** All macros, regardless of source, are automatically enabled.

As you are developing your own macros, the best balance of permissiveness and security is the second option, Disable All Macros with Notification. Select this option and then click OK. You are now ready to start creating your own macros.

Creating Macros

It makes sense that before you can use macros to enhance how you work with Excel, you need to create the macros that you'll use. (Duh!) Excel provides two ways that you can create macros—you can either record a macro or you can write one from scratch.

Regardless of how you create a macro, when you do so you always have an opportunity to specify where Excel should store the macro. You can store it in any of three places. Where you store a macro determines when it is available and how it can be later used. The following are the storage options available in Excel:

- ***Personal Macro Workbook.*** The macro is stored in a special workbook that contains only macros. This workbook is open all the time, but is hidden. The filename for this workbook is Personal.xlsb.

- ***This Workbook.*** The macro is stored as a part of the current workbook. (This is the default storage location used by Excel.)

- ***New Workbook.*** A new workbook is created and the macro is stored within it.

Remember that macros are only available if the workbook in which they are stored is open. Thus, only those stored in your Personal Macro Workbook will be available at all times. This works because the Personal Macro Workbook is always open (even if it is not visible). Macros you store in other workbooks are only available if that workbook is open.

Recording a Macro

Most people cut their teeth on macro programming by recording a series of actions so the actions can later be executed again. If you have a repetitive task that is a good candidate for a macro, you can use the macro recording capabilities of Excel to turn your actions into a macro. To record a macro, follow these steps:

1. Display the Developer tab of the ribbon.
2. Click Record Macro. Excel displays the Record Macro dialog box (see Figure 1-5).
3. In the Macro Name field, provide a name you want used for your macro. You can accept the default name, if you desire, but if you plan on using the macro more than once or twice, you will want to use a more descriptive name. (Complete details on how to name macros can be found in Chapter 3.)
4. Use the Store Macro In drop-down list to specify where you want the macro stored.
5. In the Description box you can provide an optional comment about your macro.
6. Click OK.

Excel changes the Record Macro tool, on the Developer tab, to a Stop Recording tool and starts recording everything you do. The actions you take become steps

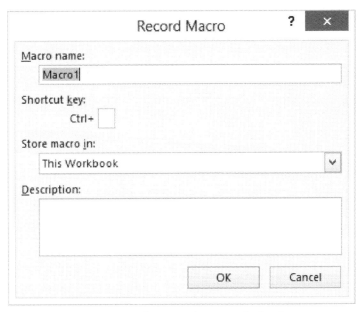

Figure 1-5. *The Record Macro dialog box.*

in the macro. When you are done performing the steps you want recorded in the macro, simply display the Developer tab of the ribbon and click the Stop Recording tool.

The steps you recorded are saved under the name you specified in step 3. You can "replay" the steps at any time, simply by running the macro again. (We'll get to how you actually run macros in just a moment.)

Relative References when Recording Macros

In the previous section you discovered how to use the macro recorder built into Excel. The recorder allows you to record your keystrokes and play them back again later. When you record your macros, Excel is very literal about recording what you do. For instance, if you start recording while cell B7 is selected and then you press the **Down Arrow** key, cell B8 is now selected.

When you later select cell E12 and play back this macro, you might expect that the macro would move down one cell, to E13, as if you had pressed the **Down Arrow** key. Instead, when that line of the macro is executed, cell B8 is selected.

The reason this happens is that Excel memorized your absolute steps. It didn't record the press of the **DOWN ARROW** key, but instead recorded the movement to cell B8. This exemplifies the default condition of the macro recorder—to record all movements and cell references absolutely.

If you instead want your macros to be recorded relatively (so that the macro moves down one cell instead of moving to cell B8), then you need to instruct Excel to do so. You do this by clicking Use Relative References on the Developer tab of the ribbon, after which all your subsequent actions are interpreted relative to the current selected cell. Click the tool a second time, and you are back to subsequent actions being interpreted absolutely.

It is important that you remember to click the appropriate tool before you take an action that is recorded. The tool's stated (on or off) affects only the recording of future actions, not what has been already recorded.

Writing a Macro from Scratch

While recording a macro can provide a quick way to begin using a macro, a much more powerful approach is to write a macro from scratch. As long as you can visualize what you want the macro to do, you can use the Visual Basic Editor to write the steps that are necessary to accomplish your task.

To create a macro from scratch, follow these steps:

1. Make sure the Developer tab of the ribbon is displayed.
2. In the Code group click the Macros tool. Excel displays the Macro dialog box, shown in Figure 1-6.

Figure 1-6. *The Macros dialog box is used to manage the macros that Excel knows about on your system.*

3. Using the Macros In drop-down list (at the bottom of the dialog box), select where you want your new macro stored.

4. In the Macro Name box, type a descriptive name you want assigned to the macro you are writing. (Complete details on how to name macros can be found in Chapter 3.) Optionally, you can enter information in the Description box.

5. Click on Create. Visual Basic for Applications starts up and you can write your macro. (Note that the Create button is only available after you complete step 4.)

6. When you are through, close the macro window by selecting the Close and Return to Microsoft Excel option from the File menu, or by pressing ALT+Q.

Running Macros

Running a macro is easy to do; you use the same Macros dialog box introduced in the previous section. If you know which macro you want to run, just follow these steps:

1. Make sure the Developer tab of the ribbon is displayed.

2. In the Code group click the Macros tool. Excel displays the Macro dialog box. (This is the same dialog box shown in Figure 1-6, except it will have any previously created macros listed within it.)

3. In the list of macros displayed in the dialog box, click once on the macro you want to run.

4. Click the Run button. Excel closes the dialog box and runs the macro you specified.

As an example, let's suppose that you record a macro named "MyMacro" using the instructions provided earlier in this chapter. When you later display the Macro dialog box (again, see Figure 1-6), you'll see "MyMacro" listed in the dialog box. All you need to do is click the macro name and then click Run. Your recorded macro is again executed on your worksheet.

While using the Macro dialog box to run macros may be easy, it can also get monotonous if you run macros quite often. If you have macros you want to run over and over, it may make more sense to have them assigned to either a keyboard shortcut or to a button somewhere on the ribbon. Once assigned to a shortcut key or a button, you can then run the macro by simply invoking the shortcut key or clicking on the button. How you assign macros to shortcut keys or ribbon buttons is discussed fully in Chapter 5.

Editing Macros

Just as surely as day follows night, at some point you'll need to edit a macro you previously recorded or wrote from scratch. Remember that all editing of macros occurs using the Visual Basic Editor. To edit an existing macro, all you need to do is follow these steps:

1. Make sure the Developer tab of the ribbon is displayed.

2. In the Code group click the Macros tool. Excel displays the Macro dialog box, shown in Figure 1-6. (You can also display the Macro dialog box by just clicking **Alt+F8**.)

3. In the list of macros displayed in the dialog box, click once on the macro you want to edit.

4. Click the Edit button. Excel closes the dialog box and displays the Visual Basic Editor with your macro displayed in the code window, as shown in Figure 1-7.

Editing an existing macro is very much like creating a new macro from scratch. The only difference is your starting point—when editing an existing macro you can see and change the code that you previously created for the macro.

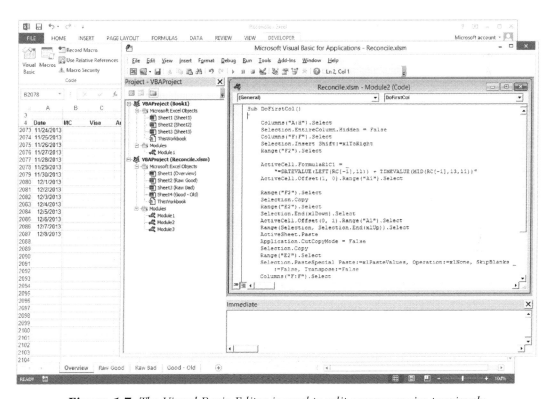

Figure 1-7. *The Visual Basic Editor is used to edit macros you've previously recorded or written.*

You can edit information in the Visual Basic Editor using many of the same editing techniques you use when working with data in your worksheets. For instance, you can select code in the window and use copy and paste commands to move the code around. You can also use the mundane editing keys (like **Backspace** and **Delete**) to make changes to the code, as necessary.

When you are done making changes to your macro, you should close the Visual Basic Editor. The easiest way is to press **Alt+Q** or choose Close and Return to Microsoft Excel from the File menu.

Deleting Macros

You'll find, over time, that many of the macros that you record or create are used for a specific purpose; they are not intended to be used over and over again for long periods of time. This means that as your needs change, you may have occasion to delete macros. To delete a macro, follow these steps:

1. Make sure the Developer tab of the ribbon is displayed.
2. In the Code group click the Macros tool. Excel displays the Macros dialog box, shown in Figure 1-6.
3. From the list of macros, select the macro you want to delete. The Delete button becomes available.
4. Click on Delete.
5. Repeat steps 3 and 4 for each macro you want to delete.
6. Click on Close when finished.

Getting Rid of the "Enable Macros" Notice

The VBA programming language included with Excel allows you to create very powerful macros. It is not uncommon to record a couple of macros for a workbook, each designed to accomplish a quick little task. When you create the macros, Excel adds what is called a module to your workbook. This module is used to store the macros that you record or create. (You actually learn more about modules in the Chapter 2.)

You may notice that every time you open a workbook that contains macros, Excel asks you if you want to enable the macros. This is part of the security system built into Excel, as described earlier in this chapter. You may also have noticed that if you delete all the macros in your workbook, Excel still asks you if you want to enable macros when you later open the workbook.

Why would Excel do this? After all, you deleted all the macros in the workbook, right? The reason is that the module automatically created by Excel to hold your macros is not automatically deleted when you get rid of the last macro—it's still there. As long as the module is there, Excel will dutifully ask you if you want to enable your macros whenever you load the workbook.

There are two ways you can overcome this problem and get rid of the macro prompt for this particular workbook. The first is to save the workbook in a non-macro format, using these steps:

1. Load the offending workbook.
2. Press **F12**. Excel displays the Save As dialog box.
3. Using the Save As Type drop-down list, choose Excel Workbook.
4. Click Save. Excel shows a dialog box that indicates, essentially, that you can't save macros in macro-free workbooks. (This is, after all, the reason you are performing these steps.)
5. Click Yes. Excel saves the workbook.

At this point you now have two workbooks whose names are essentially the same. If you examine them in a folder window, you'll see that the icon used for each of them is different.

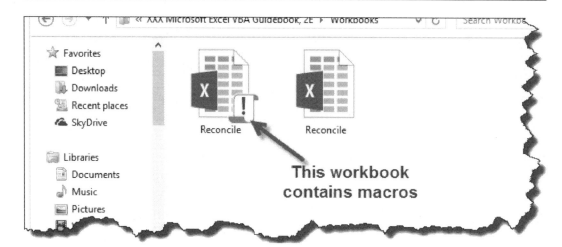

You can feel free to delete the workbook that contains macros, leaving the one that doesn't contain macros.

The other way to handle the situation and get rid of the macro prompt is to make sure that the modules that used to contain your macros are deleted. Here are the steps to follow:

1. Press ALT+F11 to display the Visual Basic Editor.

2. Near the upper-left side of the editor is the Project Explorer. This contains a hierarchical tree that shows the different modules in your workbook. If the Project Explorer is not visible on your screen, press CTRL+R to display it. (You can see the Project Explorer in Figure 1-7.)

3. Within the Project Explorer should be a folder called Modules. If it is not already open, double-click on the Modules folder to display its contents.

4. Right-click on a module in the folder. A Context menu is displayed.

5. Choose the Remove option from the Context menu. You are asked if you want to export the module before removing it.

6. Click on the No button. The module is removed.

7. Repeat steps 5 through 7 for each module in the Modules folder.

8. Close the Visual Basic Editor.

9. Resave your workbook.

At this point your workbook contains no modules, and you will not get any notification when you subsequently open it. If working with modules in this manner seems a bit confusing, don't worry—you learn more about modules and how they relate to macros in the Chapter 2.

_2_

Elements of Macros

When you first look at the programming code in a macro, you may feel lost. Don't worry; this is normal for those just beginning to work with macros. (Come on; admit it—you felt a little overwhelmed when you looked at the code for the first macro you ever recorded, didn't you?) As you spend more time with the actual code stored in macros, those feelings subside and you become more and more comfortable.

As is the case with any programming language, VBA relies upon some fundamental building blocks. A firm understanding of those building blocks can help you make sense of macros faster and create them easier. This chapter focuses upon those building blocks. Here you'll find information about each of the following:

- How projects and modules are used in macros
- Macro procedures
- Commenting macros
- Breaking up long lines in a macro
- Using objects and collections
- Understanding object methods and properties
- Using variables and operators

Projects and Modules

Visual Basic for Applications is an object-oriented programming language. This means that it understands and works with objects, as is discussed in detail later in this chapter. The highest-level object understood by VBA is known as a *project*.

For the layman non-programmer, the best way to understand a project is as a workbook. Each project (hence, each workbook) can contain other objects. Specifically, a project can contain any of the following:

- **Microsoft Excel objects.** These are objects such as workbooks. In a way, this type of object is almost circular, since a project is analogous to a workbook. However, because VBA treats these as objects, you can use programming techniques to access their internal elements, such as worksheets and cells.

- **Modules.** A module (discussed shortly) is a container for a group of related procedures (also discussed shortly). In short, a module contains your VBA programming code.

- **Class modules.** These are a special type of programming code used to define custom objects that can be used elsewhere in your programming. These are used extensively by programmers who understand the intricacies of object-oriented programming.

- **UserForm objects.** A UserForm is a custom dialog box used as an interface to a program. UserForms are considered an advanced topic, well beyond the level of beginning programmers.

- **References.** These are nothing but formal references to other projects. These are necessary when you want to *reference* objects in a different project from the current project.

The easiest way to get a handle on what constitutes a project is to user the Project Explorer, a special area visible within the Visual Basic Editor. (The Project Explorer is covered in more detail in Chapter 4.) Figure 2-1 shows an example of the Project Explorer, which displays projects and the objects within projects in a hierarchical fashion, using a tree representation.

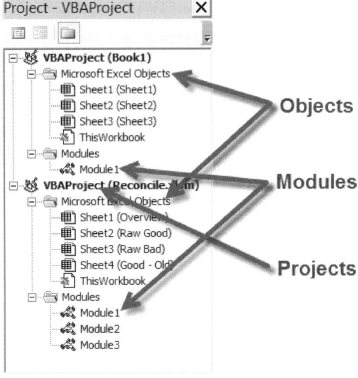

Figure 2-1. *VBA uses the concept of projects and objects extensively. The Project Explorer displays the relationship between these elements.*

For those using VBA, the most common object is known as a module. A ***module*** is a collection of programming procedures that you create. When you first record a macro, Excel places the recording into a module known as Module1. (Original name, huh?) By default this module is placed within the current workbook's project, meaning that it is available every time the current workbook is opened. You can override where macros are stored, as discussed in Chapter 3.

Understanding Procedures

The simplest definition of a procedure is a logical grouping of programming code used to accomplish one or more related tasks. (That didn't sound too formal, did it?) VBA understands two types of procedures:

- Subroutines
- Functions

Procedures are elemental, meaning that you cannot place procedures within procedures. For instance, you cannot put a subroutine within a function or within another subroutine. You can, however, execute one procedure from another procedure, as is made clear in the following sections.

Subroutines

The first type of programming procedure you can create in VBA is known as a subroutine. For instance, consider the following code:

```
Sub Macro1()
    TestSub
End Sub

Sub TestSub()
    MsgBox "In the macro"
End Sub
```

This code consists of two subroutines, Macro1 and TestSub. You can tell that these are subroutines because they start, in the first line of each procedure, with the Sub keyword. In fact, you can see that each subroutine is enclosed within two lines—the first declares the name of the subroutine using the Sub keyword and the second ends the subroutine with the End Sub statement.

In this example the Macro1 macro does nothing but call a subroutine (TestSub), which in turn displays a message in a message box. The subroutine then returns control to the main program. (You learn more about message boxes in Chapter 9.)

You can have as many subroutines in your module as you desire. The purpose of each should be to perform common, well-defined tasks so you don't have to rewrite the same code all the time. Properly used, subroutines can be very powerful.

You can increase the flexibility of your subroutines by passing parameters to them. These parameters can then be acted upon by your subroutine. For instance, consider the following macros:

```
Sub Macro1()
    A = 1
    PrintIt A
End Sub

Sub PrintIt(x)
    MsgBox x
End Sub
```

When you run Macro1, it sets a variable (A) and then passes that variable in a subroutine call to PrintIt. This PrintIt subroutine displays the value of the variable in a message box and then returns to the calling program.

Notice that the PrintIt subroutine does not use the same variable name that was used when PrintIt was invoked in the Macro1 macro. This is because VBA reassigns the value of x (what the subroutine expects to receive) so that it matches the value of A (what the program is passing to the subroutine). The important thing to remember in passing parameters to subroutines is that your program must pass the same number of parameters as the subroutine expects, and that the parameters must be of matching types and in the proper order. (The proper use of variables is discussed later in this chapter.)

Functions

The second type of procedure you can use in your programming is known as a *function*. The difference between functions and subroutines is that functions can return values, whereas subroutines cannot. Consider the following procedures:

```
Sub Macro1()
    TooMany = TestFunc
    If TooMany Then MsgBox "Too many cells selected"
End Sub

Function TestFunc() As Boolean
    TestFunc = False
    If Selection.Cells.Count > 50 Then
        TestFunc = True
    End If
End Function
```

There are two procedures in this code, one subroutine and one function. You already know how to spot the subroutine (see the previous section), and you can probably figure out that the function is named TestFunc. Note that similarly to subroutines, functions are enclosed within two lines that denote the beginning and end of the function. The keyword Function is used to declare the function and the statement End Function is used to mark the end of the function.

Take a closer look at how the function is declared in its first line:

```
Function TestFunc() As Boolean
```

The Function keyword indicates you are defining a function and giving it the name TestFunc. Note that after the parentheses you can see the keywords "As Boolean". This means that you are instructing VBA to return, from the TestFunc function, a value that uses the Boolean data type. (Data types are discussed fully later in this chapter.) Now take a look at the body of the function:

```
TestFunc = False
If Selection.Cells.Count > 50 Then
    TestFunc = True
End If
```

Note that a variable named TestFunc is set to either False or True, depending on the condition within the If … Then structure. It isn't the structure that is important at this point; that is explained fully in Chapter 7. What is important is noticing that the code assigns a value to a variable that has the same name as the function itself (TestFunc). It is the value of this variable that is returned, as a Boolean data type, when the function is completed.

This brings us back to the Macro1 macro. Note that the TestFunc function can appear on the right side of the equal sign. This makes functions very powerful and an important part of any program. VBA executes the function, returns whatever value is appropriate from that function, and assigns it to the variable on the left side of the equal sign (TooMany). The rest of the code in the Macro1 macro then acts upon the value returned.

When you create your own functions, it is often helpful to pass parameters to the function. These parameters can be used either as data that you want the function to act upon or as settings used to control how the function does its work. How you pass parameters to functions is done in much the same was as passing them to subroutines, as illustrated in the following:

```
Sub Macro1()
    A = 12.3456
    MsgBox A & "       " & RoundIt(A)
End Sub

Function RoundIt(X) As Integer
    RoundIt = Int(X + 0.5)
End Function
```

The Macro1 macro defines a number and assigns it to the variable A. It then prints that number and the result of passing the number to the RoundIt function; the output is 12.3456 and 12. Notice that the parameter should be passed to the function within parentheses.

Also notice that the function does not use the same variable name as it was passed. (The variable A is passed to the function when it is invoked; within the function this value is referred to by the variable name X.) This is because VBA reassigns the value of X (what the function needs) so it matches the value of A (what is passed to the function).

VBA allows you to specify multiple parameters to be passed to a function. The parameters simply need to be separated by commas in both the declaration of the function and whenever the function is called. The important thing to remember in passing parameters to functions is that your program must pass the same number of parameters as the function expects, and the parameters must be of matching types and in the proper order.

Procedure Scope

It should be noted that procedures (either subroutines or functions) can have a scope declared for them. By *scope* Microsoft simply means how accessible the procedure is. A procedure can either be public or private.

- A public procedure is accessible from any module in a project.
- A private procedure can be accessed only within the module in which the procedure occurs.

You declare the scope of a procedure by preceding the procedure's declaration with either the word Public or Private. The default scope for a procedure is public, so either of these declarations has exactly the same effect:

```
Public Sub UpdateMonth()
Sub UpdateMonth()
```

Because VBA assumes that all procedures are public unless declared otherwise, most programmers don't bother with the Public keyword. Instead, they simply use Private in places where they feel it is necessary:

```
Private Function EndCycle(iCycle As Integer) As String
```

You should also note that any subroutine declared Private does not appear in the Macro dialog box (invoked from the Developer tab of the ribbon). This is because Excel assumes that since you've marked it Private, you only want it available to invoke from other procedures in your project, not to be run manually by humans.

Adding Comments

Anyone who has been programming for any length of time can share a common experience: Writing a program, leaving that program for a period of time—perhaps months—and then coming back to the program and forgetting what the code is supposed to do. It is frustrating to need to go back and "decipher" what you wrote months before in order to make changes to that code.

This same thing can easily happen when you are programming macros; it is easy to forget what your program is doing or why you wrote your program. For this reason, VBA provides a way that you can add comments to your code. The comments are completely ignored by VBA, but they provide a way for you to explain anything about your code that you feel needs explaining.

Here is an example of commenting that was done in a macro:

```
Sub ConvertName()
' Replaces all instances of 'Johnson Widgets'
' with 'Johnson Widgets International'
' Make sure replacement text is blue

    'Clear any existing formatting
    Application.ReplaceFormat.Clear
```

```
    'Make replacement text bold and blue
    With Application.ReplaceFormat.Font
        .FontStyle = "Bold"
        .Color = 12611584        'Code for blue color
    End With

    'Perform the replacement
    Cells.Replace What:="Johnson Widgets", _
      Replacement:="Johnson International Widgets", _
      LookAt:=xlPart, SearchOrder:=xlByRows, _
      MatchCase:=False, SearchFormat:=False, _
      ReplaceFormat:=True
End Sub
```

Don't get bogged down in what this code actually does; that isn't important at the moment. What is important is the presence of comments within the code. Note any lines that begin with an apostrophe; these are comments. When viewed in the Visual Basic Editor (see Figure 2-2) comments appear as green text so that you can easily tell them apart from the main programming code.

If you examine this code example closely, you'll find that on some lines the apostrophe that denotes the start of a comment begins at the left margin. On some other lines it is indented a bit and on one line the apostrophe is even a few spaces to the right of some real code. The point is that VBA ignores everything after the apostrophe; it is considered a comment meant for human eyes only.

As you are programming, you'll want to make sure that you add comments liberally in your code. Doing so can help you (or others) later remember your thought process as you created your macro.

Continuing Lines

When you are creating a macro, you may run into some very long lines. VBA can handle very long lines easily, but it is usually a pain to scroll the screen left and right to review a line. Some programming languages (Such as C or Perl) allow you to continue program lines simply by pressing ENTER and continuing with the line.

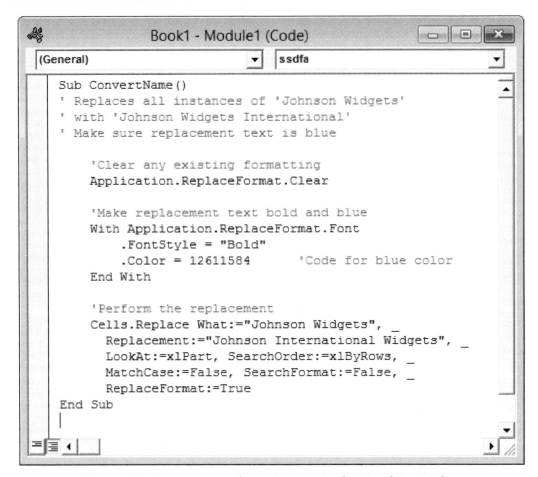

Figure 2-2. Comments are shown in green in the Visual Basic Editor.

VBA, however, requires a special character sequence to signify that you want to continue the current program line on the next. This sequence consists of a space and an underscore. Consider the following example code:

```
Cells.Replace What:="Johnson Widgets", Replacement:="Johnson International
Widgets", LookAt:=xlPart, SearchOrder:=xlByRows, MatchCase:=False,
SearchFormat:=False, ReplaceFormat:=True
```

This is a single programming statement that sets does a replacement of text. It shows on three lines in this text, but on the screen, in the Visual Basic Editor, it would be a single, very wide line. To see it all, you would need to scroll your screen to the right quite a ways.

Chapter 2: Elements of Macros

A better solution is to add the space and underscore characters strategically within the line. That informs the editor that you are actually creating a single programming statement, but that you are spreading it across multiple lines for the sake of readability. Here's an example:

```
Cells.Replace What:="Johnson Widgets", _
   Replacement:="Johnson International Widgets", _
   LookAt:=xlPart, SearchOrder:=xlByRows, _
   MatchCase:=False, SearchFormat:=False, _
   ReplaceFormat:=True
```

By now this example should look familiar—it is part of the macro code used in the preceding section. Take a look at the right side of the first four lines. The space and underscore at the end of each line signifies that the programming statement continues on the next line. You can use the continuation characters in this way to continue any programming lines you desire. The only thing you need to remember is that you can only use the characters for continuation purposes if you place them between regular tokens or keywords used in the program line. If you place them in the middle of a keyword or in a string (between quote marks), VBA won't know what you intended and may generate an error.

Variables and Operators

Most computer programs make some sort of calculation; it is a normal part of what they do. These calculations are made using variables, which are the building blocks of the calculating portion of your program. Just like different parts of a building may require different sizes of bricks, different portions of your programs require different types of variables.

Variables are nothing but a storage space for values. If you prefer real-world analogies, you can think of them as containers that hold information. They are called variables because their contents can vary, meaning they can be changed. Just as you can change what is stored inside a drinking glass, you can change what is stored within a variable.

In the following sections you learn about the different types of variables and operators you can use in VBA. One of the marks of a good programmer is the ability to match the right data type with the proper operator to produce the precise result desired. These sections teach you the fundamentals you need to increase your skills in this area.

Understanding Data Types

Variables come in different types (often called *data types*) so you can properly handle different types of information. Because VBA provides different types of variables you can use in your programs, you must learn about them so you can use them effectively. These are the data types that VBA supports:

- **Byte.** A numeric variable within the range of 0 to 255.

- **Boolean.** A variable with two possible values: True (-1) or False (0).

- **Integer.** A numeric variable designed for whole numbers in the range of -32,768 to 32,767.

- **Long.** A numeric variable designed for very large whole numbers.

- **Currency.** A numeric variable designed for calculations involving monetary values.

- **Single.** A numeric variable designed for single-precision floating-point values; accurate to about six or seven decimal places.

- **Double.** A numeric variable designed for double-precision floating-point values; accurate to about 15 decimal places.

- **Date.** A numeric variable designed to represent a date and time as a real number. The value to the left of the decimal point is the date, and that portion to the right of the decimal point is the time.

- **String.** A variable that can contain any type of text or character you desire. You can assign a maximum of approximately 2 billion characters to a string variable.

- **Object.** A variable that contains a pointer to a defined object within VBA.

- **Variant.** A variable that can contain any type of data.

An additional data type—Decimal—is also specified in the VBA documentation, but is not currently supported by the language. (It is doubtful it will ever be supported, since VBA has been around for over a decade now without any change in the specification or lack of support.)

In order to make sure that your variable matches the type of data that you plan on storing in it, you should explicitly declare your variables near the beginning of your procedures. You do so by using the Dim keyword, in this manner:

```
Dim iMyInteger As Integer
```

The Dim keyword is followed by the name you want to use for the variable, the As keyword, and then the data type you want used for the variable. In this example, iMyInteger is the variable name. There is nothing special about this name, and I choose to put the "i" in front of it so that later I remember that the variable is an integer. I similarly preface other variable names with characters that indicate what data type I used for the variable.

Most of the VBA data types should be fairly self-explanatory, but there are a few that require special attention so you can understand them fully. These are examined in the following sections.

The Date Data Type

Dates and times are both stored in the Date data type using a serial number technique. The serial number consists of whole numbers (those to the left of the decimal point) that represent the number of days since January 1, 100 (yes, the year 100). Thus, 0 is the serial number for January 1, 100; 1 is the serial number for January 2, 100; 2 is for January 3, 100; and so on. These serial numbers increment all the way through whatever huge number represents December 31, 9999. The portion to the right of the decimal point in the serial number represents the fraction of a day represented by the serial number.

The easiest way to set a Date variable is to use the following technique:

```
dMyDate = #4/15/2014#
```

When you enclose the date within two hash marks (number signs), VBA understands that it should be considered a date. You can also use two special VBA functions to assign dates, as shown here:

```
dMyDate = DateSerial(2014, 4, 15)
dMyDate = CDate("4/15/2014")
```

The first function (DateSerial) converts a year, month, and day into a date serial number. The second function (CDate) converts a text string into a date.

The Object Data Type

Objects are part and parcel of an object-oriented programming language such as Visual Basic for Applications; they are discussed more fully later in this chapter. They are used to access all the pieces and parts that Excel is capable of working with in a workbook. The most likely time that you'll utilize objects is when you want to work with an object within Excel's object model hierarchy.

The Variant Data Type

The Variant data type gets its name from its ability to vary its format, taking on the form of the data it contains. If you store a string in a variant, the variant appears as a String data type and can be manipulated by the String operators. If you store a number to a variant, it acts like a numeric variable and you can use the arithmetic operators in its manipulation.

While variants are convenient, in the sense that you don't have to think much to use them, I recommend that unless you have a specific need which can't be solved in any reasonable way without their use, you should avoid them. It's always better to have a thorough understanding of what your program is doing and why it is doing it. Using variants is like painting without first scraping, sanding, and priming. If everything under the new paint is OK you can get away without any extra work. If it's not, then the new paint is soon a mess and you are doing the job over.

Understanding Operators

Variables are the raw material of your programs. You work with that raw material using operators. Fortunately, VBA has a rich set of operators available. This operator set makes the job of programming much simpler.

As mentioned earlier in this chapter, variables are so named because their value can change—they can vary. This flexibility is the feature which makes them so useful. There are many ways to change the value contained in a variable.

When working with variables, the kind of manipulation you perform is defined by the operator. An *operator* is the symbol that defines what type of operation should take place in an equation. If there is only one variable being operated on, it is called the operand. If there is more than one variable, they are referred to collectively as the operands.

Arithmetic Operators

The most common category of operations is those involving arithmetic. You probably know most of the arithmetic operations, as they are routinely used when creating formulas in Excel. However, VBA includes some useful operations you may not be familiar with. You probably already are familiar with + (addition), - (subtraction), * (multiplication), and / (division). Other arithmetic operators that may be more esoteric to you are ^ (exponentiation), \ (integer division), and Mod (modulus).

The exponentiation operator (the caret character, or Sнift+6 on the keyboard) is used to raise a number to a power. For instance, 2*2 is noted as 2^2 and 2*2*2 is noted as 2^3. You also can raise a number to a fractional exponent, as in 3 ^ 1.5. VBA can also handle numbers raised to negative exponents.

Integer division, represented by the backslash operator, takes two values as operands and returns an integer as the result. If you use a non-integer as one or both of the operands, the non-integer is converted to an integer first and then the division is performed. The result is always an integer. Be careful not to confuse integer division with normal division, which is represented by a forward slash. Each type of division produces different results.

The modulus operator (Mod) hearkens back to the days when you were first learning to divide. The answer you got to a problem such as "six divided by five" was "one remainder one". The remainder is what is left over after the division. The Mod operator returns the remainder of a division operation. Just like with the integer division operator, the operands are rounded to integers prior to the Mod operation being performed. Also, as with integer division, the result is always an integer.

There's an important (although tangential) distinction to make here when it comes to the Mod operator. If you've spent any time creating Excel formulas, you probably know that Excel includes a MOD worksheet function. Don't confuse the Mod VBA operator with the MOD worksheet function—they behave quite differently. In VBA the Mod operator really does work with integers, but in Excel the MOD worksheet function can work with floating point numbers. This can lead to very different results. For instance, try the following in VBA:

```
Sub TestMod()
    Dim j As Integer

    j = 19.9 Mod 6.6
    MsgBox j
End Sub
```

If you run the macro, the result displayed is 6, which is the remainder after doing the integer division. VBA automatically rounds the first operand to 20 and the second operand to 7, and the remainder of dividing 20 by 7 is 6. However, if you use the formula =MOD(19.9,6.6) in an Excel worksheet, the result is 0.1—a far cry from the result in VBA.

Comparison Operators

The comparison operators are used when you want to know the magnitude of one variable compared to another. "Does variable1 contain a value which is larger, smaller, or exactly equal to variable2?" is the kind of question to which a comparison operator provides an answer.

The result of any comparison can only be True or False. In addition, comparison operators can be used on either numeric values or text values. The six comparison operators are as follows:

- = (equal)
- < (less than)
- > (greater than)

- <= (less than or equal)
- >= (greater than or equal)
- <> (not equal)

The equal operator is fairly straightforward. Just remember that equal means exactly equal. If two values differ by even the slightest amount, they are not evaluated as equal. The two values 4.0 and 4.0000000001 may look the same when displayed by your VBA programming (due to formatting), but the values in memory are different and therefore not equal.

When using the Greater Than and Less Than operators remember that any negative number is less than any positive number. This is easy to remember if you picture all numbers placed on a number line, like you used to use in elementary school. The line has 0 in the middle, the positive numbers (1,2,3, and so on) to the right, and the negative numbers (-1, -2, -3, and so on) heading off to the left. Pick any two numbers on this number line. The one on the left is always less and the one to the right is always more.

The Not Equal operator tells you if any two variables are different, even by the slightest amount. Not Equal can be used to determine if two dates or times are the same, if two files have identical names, or if the length of two files differ. It can be used anywhere you need to know if there is the slightest difference.

Less Than or Equal combines two questions into one. "Is value1 less than value2" OR "is value1 equal to value2". OR is shown in capitals to emphasize that if either of the conditions is met, the statement is True. Greater Than or Equal works in a similar (but opposite) manner.

Logical Operators

You use logical operators to build more complex logical constructs. For example, if you have a group of individuals and you want to locate all single red-headed males who are between the ages of 20 and 30 and who don't have a pet, logical operators provide the means. The following demonstrates:

```
(Married = "S") And (Hair = "Red") And (Age >= 20) And (Age <= 30) And (Pet
= "None")
```

Logical operators allow you to apply Boolean logic to your data, determining a final solution that is either True or False. VBA provides the following logical operators:

- And
- Or
- Xor (exclusive Or)
- Eqv (equivalent)
- Imp (implication)
- Not (or the logical opposite of)

Normally VBA's logical operators are used in some sort of logical construct, such as an If ... Then construct. A full discussion of these constructs is provided in Chapter 7, but a quick overview is provided in the examples here.

The And operator returns a True value only if both operands are True, otherwise the result if False. Here is an example of using the operator:

```
If (FirstName = "Tony") And (LastName = "Carpenter") Then
    MsgBox "Found Tony"
Else
    MsgBox "Tony could not be found!"
End If
```

Notice the use of parentheses in the example. Operations within parentheses are performed first and then the results are used in further calculations. This ensures that operations are performed in the order you intend. In the example above, FirstName is compared with "Tony" and LastName is compared with "Carpenter", then the results are compared.

The Or operator returns a True value if either of the operands are True. It only returns a False value if both of the operands are False:

```
If FirstName = "Beth" Or FirstName = "Ginger" Then
    MsgBox "Female"
End If
```

The Xor operator returns a True value when only one of the operands is True. It returns a False value whenever both operands are the same, whether they are both True or both False. Here is an example:

```
If (FirstName = "Tony") Xor (LastName = "Carpenter") Then
    MsgBox "Same first name or same last name but not both."
Else
    MsgBox "None with just the same first or last name."
End If
```

The Eqv operator returns a True value only if both operands are equal, otherwise the result is False. Here is an example:

```
If FirstName Eqv LastName Then
    DoError          'Signify error condition
End If
```

In all numeric situations the Eqv operator is the same as using an equal sign in a comparison. Eqv does not act as a comparison operator for strings, however.

The Imp operator is the local implication operator. It returns a False value only if the second operand is False and the first is True, otherwise the result is True:

```
If (Price > 100000) Imp (Pay > 60000) Then
    MsgBox "Applicant doesn't qualify"     'Pay not high enough
Else
    MsgBox "Applicant appears to qualify"
End If
```

The Not operator differs from the other logical operators in that it does not require two operands. Instead, it performs a logical negation of a value. In other words, a True value is changed to False and vice versa. Here's an example of how you could use the Not operator in an equation:

```
If Not (PayLevel > 1000) Then
    MsgBox "Pay is very low for this job."
End If
```

String Operators

Earlier you learned about comparison operators and how they can be used to compare numeric values. Comparison operators also can be used with strings, and then the result used in further computations. In addition, VBA provides a way to concatenate (combine) strings together. Consider the following code fragment, which continues on the next page:

```
sFirstName = "John"
sLastName = "Davis"
```

```
sFullName = sFirstName & " " & sLastName
sSortName = sLastName & ", " & sFirstName
```

When this code is executed, the sFullName variable contains the characters "John Davis" and the sSortName variable contains "Davis, John".

You'll find that strings and string operations are involved in virtually every program you can imagine.

Using Objects and Collections

As mentioned earlier, Visual Basic for Applications is an object-oriented programming language. This means that it works with objects and collections of objects. This may sound a bit odd, but it is no different than us as humans—we work with objects, as well.

Consider your home for a moment; it contains many objects and collections of objects. For instance, if you walk into your kitchen you may find a dish on the counter. This dish is a single object, but it is also a member of a larger collection of objects referred to as dishes. You can do things with the single dish (just like VBA can do things with a single object) or you or you can do things with the entire collection of dishes (just like VBA can do things with a collection of objects).

In the following section you get a quick introduction to the way that VBA works with Excel's available objects and object collections.

Excel's Object Model

You may consider it a rather obvious statement to say that Excel allows you to work with worksheets. It is, after all, a spreadsheet program. While you may intuitively understand what a worksheet is, VBA does not; remember that it can only do work with objects. Fortunately, Excel makes certain objects accessible to VBA and allows them to be worked with. Worksheets are an example of the type of objects that Excel makes available to VBA.

In fact, there are many, many different types of objects that Excel makes available. All of these objects, taken together, are referred to as Excel's *object model*. If you understand just a bit about this model, then you'll start to understand how you can access, modify, and otherwise use the various objects available to Excel and to VBA.

There are literally hundreds of different objects that Excel allows you to access through VBA. To get an idea of what objects are available, take a look at Excel's help system for VBA. The specific steps you follow to use the help system depends on the version of Excel you are using. (Microsoft is notorious for changing up how their help system works from version to version.)

Finding Object Model Help in Excel 2013

If you are using Excel 2013, finding help on the Excel object model can be an exercise in detective work. Here's what I needed to do on one of my systems:

1. Display the Visual Basic Editor. (The easiest way is to simply press **ALT+F11** while in Excel.)

2. With the Visual Basic Editor visible, press **F1**. Excel displays the help system for VBA, as shown in Figure 2-3.

3. From this point on you need to do a bit of detective work because Microsoft might have deposited you on a different starting page. On the one shown in Figure 2-3, you should click the large "Welcome to the Visual Basic for Applications Language Reference for Office 2013" link. The options in the Navigation bar, at the left of the browser window, change.

4. In the Navigation bar, click Office 2013 (not Office 2013 Shared). You'll see additional options appear under that link.

5. Click Excel 2013. More options appear.

6. Click Excel 2013 Developer Reference. (Still more options.)

7. Click Object Model. Your screen should appear similar to what you see in Figure 2-4.

Each of the topics listed in the Navigation bar, under the Object Model option, is an object available in Excel. Scroll through them; you'll discover hundreds of different objects. You can figure out the purpose of most of the objects just

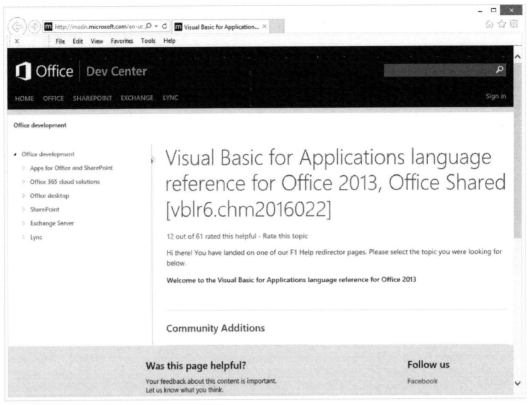

***Figure 2-3.** The VBA help system screen that you see could vary, depending on several factors including the phase of the moon.*

by looking at their names. For instance, you can probably figure out that the AutoCorrect object represents an AutoCorrect entry accessible within Excel.

If you want additional information on other objects, just click on them in the Navigation bar. You'll then see, at the right side of the browser window, a good overview of that particular object.

Finding Object Model Help in Excel 2010

Remember me saying that Microsoft is notorious on changing how the help system works from version to version? It's true; in Excel 2010 you follow an entirely different set of steps to get help about the object model:

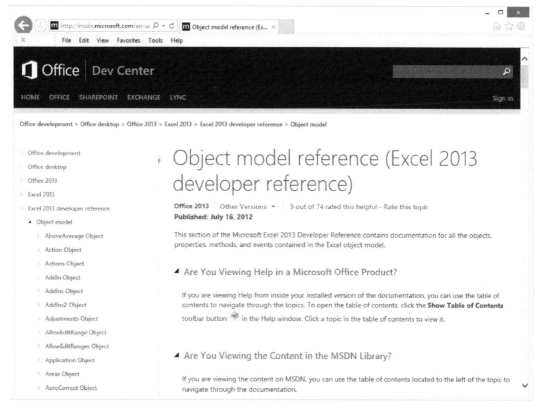

Figure 2-4. *Finding information about Excel objects can be an exercise in detective work.*

1. Display the Visual Basic Editor. (The easiest way is to simply press **ALT+F11** while in Excel.)

2. With the Visual Basic Editor visible, press **F1**. Excel displays the help system for VBA.

3. On the main screen for the help system, click the Excel 2010 Developer Reference link.

4. Click the Reference link. What you see should be similar to what is shown in Figure 2-5.

Each of the topics listed in the Subcategories section is an object available in Excel. Scroll through them; you'll discover hundreds of different objects. You can figure out the purpose of most of the objects just by looking at their names.

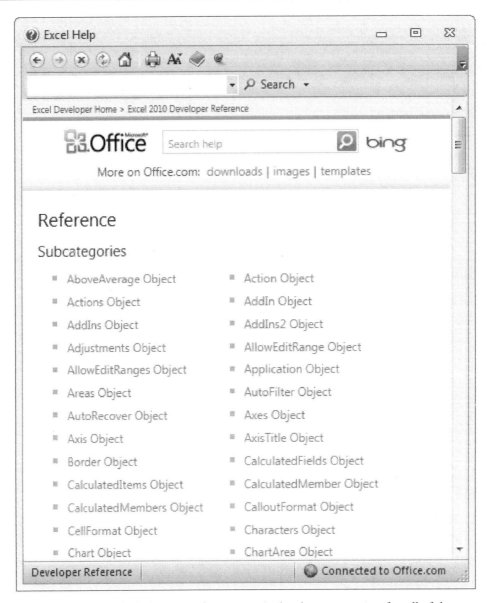

Figure 2-5. *The help system for VBA provides documentation for all of the objects in Excel's object model.*

For instance, you can probably figure out that the Worksheet object represents a worksheet in your workbook.

Finding Object Model Help in Older Excel Versions

The preceding two sections focused on how to find Excel object model help in the two latest versions of Excel. If you are using an older version, the steps you follow are going to be different. (Why Microsoft keeps changing the steps, I don't know. Must be a well-paid but underworked department in the company in charge of this area.)

Regardless of the version you are using, though, the first couple of steps are going to be the same: display the Visual Basic Editor (Alt+F11) and then display the help system (F1). It is from that point forward that you will need to poke around and try different options. Just look for anything remotely related to the object model, which is generally included within a "programmer's reference" or "developer's reference."

Exploring Excel's Objects

Once you find the list of objects in the help system, take some time to look through them. Don't let the sheer number of objects overwhelm you, however. As you work in the Visual Basic Editor, you'll find that it is quite helpful—regardless of the version of Excel you are using—on suggesting the names of objects that you may want to work with. (This becomes apparent as you start to type VBA statements into the editor.)

In reality, you'll find that you only work with a handful of different objects. These are the objects that you'll probably work with the most:

- **Application.** This object is the top-level object in Excel. It is called the Application object because it represents the currently running version of Excel. Every other object belongs to the Application object.

- **Workbook.** You can probably figure out that a Workbook object represents a single Excel workbook. This is a workbook that is open within the program; it is not an unopened workbook on your hard drive. Workbook objects belong to the Application object and they can contain many other types of objects.

- **Worksheet.** You know from working with Excel that workbooks contain worksheets. In VBA you use the Worksheet object to refer to a single worksheet within a Workbook object.

- **Range.** This is a very common object that belongs to many higher-level objects. It represents the entirety of whatever object to which it belongs and it functions as a "gateway" that allows you to access various members of the higher-level object.

- **Selection.** This object represents whatever is selected within the worksheet at the time that the macro is running.

Grouping Similar Objects Together

Excel automatically groups similar objects together into what are called *collections*. For instance, individual Worksheet objects are grouped together in the Worksheets collection and individual Shape objects are grouped in the Shapes collection.

If you examine objects in Excel's object model (see Figure 2-2), take note of the plural object names: Actions, AddIns, AllowEditRanges, Axes, CalculatedItems, CalculatedMembers, etc. Each of these is a collection of individual objects. VBA allows you to access individual members of collections or to work with an entire collection.

Assigning Objects to Variables

Earlier in this chapter you learned about how VBA works with variables. When you are working with the various objects in Excel's object model, you'll often find it helpful to assign an object to a variable. This makes it easier in the program to later work with the various members of the object. (Object members are described in the next section.)

To assign an object to a variable, you use the Set keyword. For example, you might want to work with the range B3:E7 within a worksheet. You can define the variable you are going to use for this purpose in this manner:

```
Dim rMyRange As Range
```

When you later want to assign the actual object for the cell range to the variable, you do so with this statement:

```
Set rMyRange = Worksheets("Annual Budget").Range("B3:E7")
```

This assigns the Range object for B3:E7 of the worksheet named "Annual Budget" to the rMyRange variable. (That's a mouthful, huh?) This variable now contains the Range object and you can access that object using the variable at any time. Essentially, the rMyRange variable contains those cells (B3:E7) of the worksheet.

If you later no longer need to reference the rMyRange object, you can use the Set keyword to get rid of the variable in this manner:

```
Set rMyRange = Nothing
```

Understanding Object Members

Objects or collections of objects can have a number of different members that belong to them. These members are of two primary types: methods and properties. It is important to understand more about these members, as they represent the "meat and bones" of working with objects.

Doing Operations with Methods

The easiest way to look at a method is as some sort of process that Excel allows you to perform using an object. For instance, you might want your macro to create a new worksheet. You do this by using the Add method for the Worksheets collection, in this manner:

```
Worksheets.Add Before:=Worksheets(1)
```

Note that you separate the object name (in this case Worksheets) from the method name (Add) by a single period. When this line is executed, VBA dutifully adds a new, empty worksheet to the collection of worksheets in the current workbook. In this case, the new worksheet is added before the first worksheet in the collection, so it's worksheet tab will appear to the left of any other worksheet tabs in the workbook. The period between "Worksheets" and "Add" is used to specify a movement down a level in the hierarchy of Excel's object model. As you move from left to right on the line, each period you encounter represents another movement through the hierarchy.

The number and type of methods available for an object depends on the nature of the object to which the methods belong. For instance, the Hyperlink object possesses a Follow method that is used to display the target of that hyperlink. It doesn't make sense that the Follow method would be available with other objects, such as a Worksheet or a FormatCondition (an object that referes to a conditional format).

Working with Properties

Each object in the Excel object model possesses a group of ***properties***. These are nothing but attributes or characteristics that belong to or describe the object. For instance, in real life if you are looking at a dish in your kitchen, its characteristics might be its diameter, its depth, its color, or any number of other descriptors. These are, in the object-oriented world, properties of the object.

As an example, an Axis is used to control how a particular axis of a chart appears. An Axis object has a good number of properties, such as AxisTitle, CrossesAt, HasMajorGridlines, Height, and many more. In total, there are over 40 different properties associated with an Axis object. They describe characteristics of the axis, in exquisite detail.

When creating programming statements in VBA, you refer to properties using the same technique that you refer to methods. For instance, suppose you wanted to assign the text of a particular cell to a string variable:

```
sRawText = Worksheets("Annual Budget").Range("B3").Text
```

After this statement is executed, the sRawText variable contains what is in cell B3, as displayed in the Excel worksheet. As described earlier in the chapter, you can assign an object (such as the cell in a worksheet) to a variable and then later use that variable to reference the properties of the object represented by the variable, in this manner:

```
Set rMyRange = Worksheets("Annual Budget").Range("B3")
```

```
sRawText = rMyRange.Text
```

An important concept about properties is that some of them can be written into (you can change them) and some properties can only be read. You'll discover which properties are of which type by trial and error and by examining the online documentation for each property.

Finally, it is important to understand that some properties are fully objects in their own right. Consider the following programming statement:

```
sCellStyle = Worksheets("Annual Budget").Range("B3").Style
```

This line sets the sCellStyle variable equal to the name of the style associated with cell B3 in the Annual Budget worksheet. In this instance, the primary object is Worksheets("Annual Budget"), which is the first worksheet of that name in the current workbook. Everything after that point is considered a property of that primary object. Thus, Range("B3") is a property of the primary object, even though it is an object in its own right. The Style property is simply that—a property of the object/property that precedes it in the hierarchy.

Making Sense of Members

Since there are hundreds of different objects available in the Excel object model, there are thousands of different methods provided to work with those objects and even more properties for those objects. It is impossible for a human to keep track of that number of methods and properties, so it is fortunate that the Visual Basic Editor provides some help for you, automatically.

Remember that it was noted earlier that periods are used to denote movement through Excel's object model hierarchy. Thus, the following statement, which uses two periods, denotes the movement through several layers of the hierarchy:

```
sCellStyle = Worksheets("Annual Budget").Range("B3").Style
```

As you start typing statements into the Visual Basic Editor, every time you type a period you'll see a list of options based upon the level of the hierarchy you are currently traversing. The options are shown in a drop-down list of members, with an indicator as to whether the member is a method or property, as shown here:

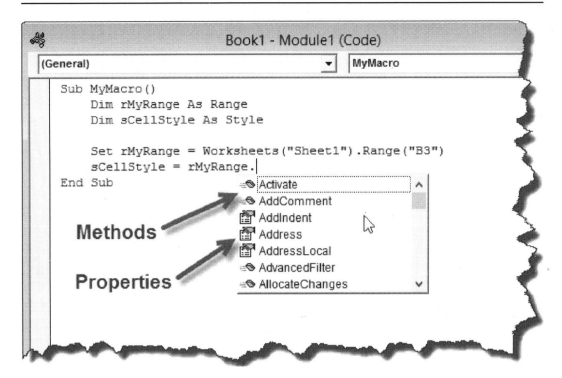

Note that the drop-down list of members is dynamic; it always changes depending on what is possible to come next, based upon the hierarchy of Excel's object model.

VBA Constants

Besides variables (which you already learned about), VBA also allows you to work with constants. Remember that variables are called such because they can vary. Similarly, constants are called such because they remain constant; they don't vary. In VBA constants are of three types: literal, symbolic, or enums.

Using Literal Constants

Literal constants are very simple in nature. You can use them on the right side of most any operator. The following is, perhaps, the simplest example possible of using literal constants:

```
X = 2 + 3
```

Obviously this formula ends up in the variable X being equal to 5, but it is not X on which you should focus. Both 2 and 3 are constants—they don't change. Constants can also be text strings, in which case they are surrounded by quote marks:

```
sMyString = "abc" & " " & "def"
```

In this instance there are three constants, each surrounded by quote marks that are concatenated together and assigned to the sMyString variable.

Finally, you can also enclose date and time constants with hash marks or number signs:

```
dMyDate = #6/11/2013#
```

Creating Symbolic Constants

Symbolic constants are similar to variables in that they are declared within a program and given a name (a symbolic name, if you prefer) that can subsequently be used in the program. Consider the following example:

```
Const sMyName = "Allen Wyatt"
```

The Const keyword tells VBA that you are setting up a constant. It is followed by the name you want used for this constant (sMyName), the equal sign, and the value you want used for the constant. If you later use the name sMyName in your coding, then VBA knows that you really mean "Allen Wyatt".

As mentioned earlier, the values of constants cannot change within your program once they are set. If you try to change the value of a constant, VBA generates an error. For instance, if your program included the constant declaration above, then the following line elsewhere in your program would generate an error:

```
sMyName = "Somebody else"
```

Excel's Enumerations

The third type of constant is more correctly known as an *enumeration*, or enum for short. Don't let the fancy name fool you; these are nothing but system-defined symbolic constants. VBA provides a wide variety of enums (somewhere in excess of 700 of them) that are used for a wide variety of things. For instance, the enum vbCrLf is a constant for the ASCII codes for a carriage return and a line feed:

```
MsgBox "You made a mistake" & vbCrLf & "Try again"
```

VBA enums always start with the lowercase letters *vb* (as in vbCrLf or vbTab). If you see some enums that start with the lowercase letters *xl* (as in xlHairline or xlThick), that means that the enum is a part of Excel's object model. Excel provides somewhere around a few thousand different enumeration constants for its object model.

As you work through the examples provided in this book, you'll often find references to the built-in enumerations. And, as you develop your skills with VBA, you'll find yourself relying on them quite a bit. Why? Because doing so is easier than figuring out the number that the enumeration replaces. It also provides a bit of insurance in case Microsoft, unbeknownst to us mere mortals, decides to change the behind-the-scenes numbers. Using the enumeration, whenever possible, means that even if Microsoft makes a change, your program will still work as expected.

3

What's In a Name?

One of the first tasks you need to figure out how to do when working with macros is to figure out what to name them. It isn't as trivial of a task as it may seem, however. Names of macros are very important, and this chapter is designed to help you understand all the ins and outs of the names you may consider.

In this chapter you discover the following:

- How to create your own macro names
- How to rename an existing macro
- Where your macros are stored
- Understanding event handlers
- Excel's special automatic macros

Naming Macros

Whenever you choose to create a macro (see Chapter 1) you'll need to come up with a name for that macro. VBA is fairly flexible in allowing you to name your macros. In fact, there are only three simple rules you need to follow:

- Your macro names must start with a letter, after which they can contain letters, numbers, and underscores.

- Your macro names must not contain any spaces, symbols (except the underscore), or punctuation marks.
- Macro names must not be longer than 80 characters.

If you try to use a macro name that violates these three rules, you'll see an error message displayed and have the opportunity to correct your violation. In order to make sure your macros are as usable as possible, you'll want to make sure that the name you use is clear, descriptive, and only as long as it needs to be to avoid confusion.

It is also a good idea to not use a macro name that matches any existing VBA function or enum. (Functions and enumerations are discussed in Chapter 2.) If you do so the results may be unpredictable.

One good idea is to make sure that your macros all start with some unique letter sequence that makes sense for your system. For instance, you may want to start all your macros with your three initials. Doing so allows you to easily differentiate those macros you created from any other macros that may be on your system. Plus, it is unlikely that your initials conflict with the start of any of Excel's or VBA's built-in features.

Renaming Macros

At its heart a macro is nothing more than a series of instructions you want the computer to execute. It is a program that is run in the framework provided by Excel. As you create macros, you'll probably come across a need to rename a few of the macros you previously created. To do this it's easiest to work with the Visual Basic Editor. Follow these steps:

1. Press ALT+F11. Excel displays the Visual Basic Editor.
2. In the Code window, use the Procedure drop-down list to choose the procedure you want to rename. The procedure you select is displayed in the window.
3. At the top of the macro you'll see the procedure definition, consisting of the word "Sub" or Function followed by the name of the macro. Change the actual name in this line. (Don't change the keywords Sub

or Function or the space that follows the keywords Sub or function, and don't change anything starting with the left parenthesis that follows the name of the procedure.)

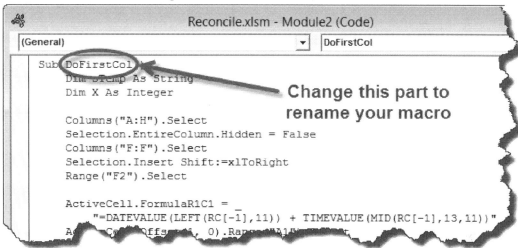

4.   Close the Visual Basic Editor.

That's it; the macro is now renamed to whatever name you used in step 3.

If you change the name of a function that you previously created, you'll also want to search through the rest of your project and see if your function is called from any of your other code. Changing the name of the function by following the above steps doesn't change any code that calls the old name; you need to do that manually. If you don't make these changes, then you'll get an error whenever you try to run a macro that references the old function name.

Where Macros are Stored

You know where Excel stores your workbooks—on your hard drive or on some other storage medium, such as a flash drive. Macros, though, aren't stored in dedicated files in this manner. Instead, macros are stored as part of other files, much like graphics or text boxes are stored as part of a different file (workbook files).

Early in Chapter 2 you learned about modules and how VBA procedures are stored in those modules. You can store VBA modules with some types of Excel workbooks, but not with all of them. In fact, when you save an Excel workbook, Excel changes the filename extension based on whether there is a VBA module in the file:

- **XLSX.** This is a regular Excel workbook that doesn't contain any macros.

- **XLSM.** This is a regular Excel workbook that contains at least one VBA module.

- **XLTX.** This is an Excel template that doesn't contain any macros.

- **XLTM.** This is an Excel template that contains at least one VBA module.

You can specify where you want to store your macros by using the controls available when you first create the macro.

Specifying a Location when Recording a Macro

In Chapter 1 you discovered how easy it is to record a series of actions as a macro. What you may not have realized was that as part of the recording process Excel gives you the chance to specify where you want to save the macro you are recording. To see where this occurs, start by displaying the Developer tab of the ribbon. Then click the Record Macro tool in the Code group. Excel displays the Record Macro dialog box, shown in Figure 3-1.

Note that the dialog box includes a drop-down list called Store Macro In. If you click this list, Excel provides a number of options for you. The top option is always Personal Macro Workbook. If stored in this location, your macro will be available at all times while using Excel. This is not the default choice, however; you need to select this option if that is where you want your macro stored.

The other options available in the drop-down list depend on how you are using Excel at the moment. Basically you'll see an option in the list for each workbook or template open in Excel. Excel even provides options for all the non-macro-enabled workbooks and templates; those that end with the XLSX or

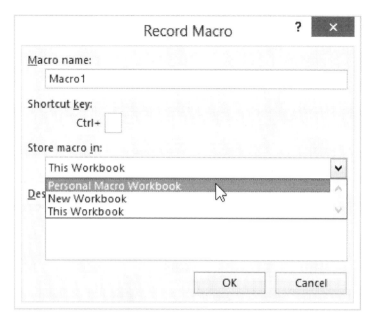

Figure 3-1. When recording a macro you can specify where the macro is to be stored by using the Store Macro In drop-down list.

XLTX filename extensions. If you choose one of these as the place where your macro should be stored, then the next time you chose to save that workbook or template, Excel asks you to save it using the XLSM or XLTM extensions.

Specifying a Location when Creating a Macro from Scratch

Choosing where Excel stores your from-scratch macros is similar to choosing where it saves your recorded macros. The biggest difference is that you make the selection in the Macro dialog box instead of the in the Record Macro dialog box. The easiest way to display this dialog box is to simply press **ALT+F8**. You can then click the Macros In drop-down list to see places where macros can be stored (see Figure 3-2).

If you compare Figure 3-2 with what is shown in Figure 3-1, you can probably figure out how the various options correlate with each other. It is interesting to note that the wording of the available options is different, even though they do the same things. Basically the meaningful options are as follows:

Figure 3-2. *When creating a macro from scratch you can specify where the macro is to be stored by using the Macros In drop-down list.*

- **All Open Workbooks.** This means that the macro is stored in the Personal Macro Workbook and is available to all workbooks at all times in Excel.

- **This Workbook.** This is the currently open workbook; the one active at the time you displayed the Macro dialog box.

- **Templates.** Any currently open templates are available in the drop-down list.

- **Workbooks.** Each of your currently open workbooks is available in the drop-down list.

Choose where you want your macro stored, and once you click on Create then Excel opens the Code window for the appropriate module in that template or workbook.

Event Handlers

Objects within Excel can have events handlers associated with them. An event handler is a special type of macro that is triggered (executed) automatically whenever a particular event occurs. There are a wide range of events which Excel can recognize, as you'll soon discover.

Event handlers have special names, defined by VBA and Excel. You modify what Excel does when an event is triggered by finding the event handler and providing the series of VBA steps that should be executed whenever that event is triggered. Most event handlers are associated with the special ThisWorkbook and Worksheet objects, which exist for every workbook and worksheet you create in Excel. (You'll discover more about the various names for event handlers later in this section.)

When an event that triggers an event handler occurs, some of the events (but not all of them) can pass values to the handler, the same as parameters can be passed to your own macro procedures. These values, which are built into the event declarations, can be accessed and in some cases changed within the event handler you create.

Avoiding Problems with Event Handlers

It is important to understand that since events are triggered automatically, it is possible that events can be triggered while your programming code is handling the occurrence of a previous event. Most of the time this isn't a problem; Excel handles each event in turn, as necessary. It becomes a problem, however, if something you do within an event handler triggers the exact same event handler again.

For instance, one event handler (Worksheet_Change) is triggered whenever a cell within a worksheet changes. You might, within your programming code for the event handler, make a change in the worksheet. Your change triggers the event handler again, which makes another change, which triggers the event handler again, etc. This can easily result in an endless loop that hangs up your macro and may crash Excel.

To avoid such potential problems, you'll want to modify the EnableEvents property, in the following manner:

```
Private Sub Worksheet_Change(ByVal Target As Range)
    Application.EnableEvents = False
    Range("C14").Value = "Purple Widgets"
    Application.EnableEvents = True
End Sub
```

Note that the EnableEvents property is set to False just before the change is made in cell C14, and then set to True just after the change. This stops Excel from recognizing and responding to events during the critical phase of your handler—while the cell value is being changed.

It is important that if you turn off event handling in this manner that you remember to turn it back on. Failure to do so results in Excel, for the rest of your session, ignoring all the events it would have otherwise recognized.

Event Handlers and Workbooks

To see what events are available for a workbook, follow these steps:

1. Press **ALT+F11** to display the Visual Basic Editor.

2. Note the Project Explorer window, at the left side of the editor. (The Project Explorer is explained in more detail in Chapter 4.) If the Project Explorer window is not visible for some reason, press **CTRL+R** to display it.

3. Note that the Project Explorer shows each workbook you have open as a project. Locate the workbook (project) for which you want to create an event handler.

4. Double-click the ThisWorkbook object, in the Project Explorer, for the workbook you located. (See Figure 3-3.) A code window for the workbook is opened.

5. Click the Object down-arrow (see Figure 3-4) and choose Workbook.

6. Click the Procedure down-arrow (see Figure 3-4) to see the events that can be handled for the workbook.

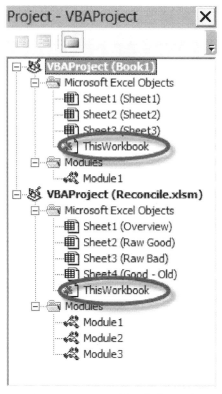

Figure 3-3. *Double-clicking the ThisWorkbook object opens a code window for that object.*

Note in Figure 3-4 that Excel created, automatically, an event handler named Workbook_Open. There are many other events that are available in the dropdown list, as follows:

- **Workbook_Activate.** This event is triggered when the workbook is activated (selected so that it receives focus).

- **Workbook_AddinInstall.** Workbooks can be saved, in Excel, so that they function as add-ins. If you save a workbook as an addin, and then install that add-in within Excel, this event is triggered. (Helpful for adding activation coding for an add-in.)

- **Workbook_AddinUninstall.** If you create an add-in from a workbook, install that add-in in Excel, and then later uninstall it,

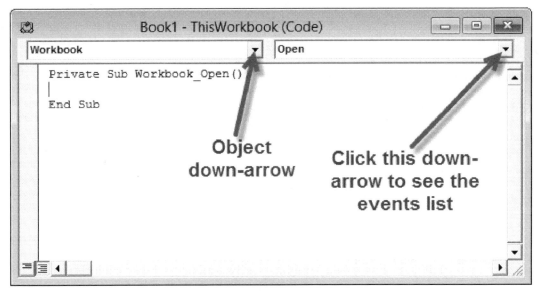

Figure 3-4. Clicking the Procedure down-arrow shows a list of events available for the Workbook object.

this event is triggered just before the add-in is uninstalled. (Helpful for removing configuration changes initially made by the add-in.)

- **Workbook_AfterSave.** This event is triggered right after a workbook's file has been saved on a disk.

- **Workbook_AfterXmlExport.** This event is triggered after a workbook is saved in XML format or workbook data is exported in XML format.

- **Workbook_AfterXmlImport.** This event is triggered when new XML data is imported into a workbook or when an XML data connection is refreshed.

- **Workbook_BeforeClose.** This event is triggered when a workbook is closed; it is the opposite of the Workbook_Open event.

- **Workbook_BeforePrint.** This event is triggered immediately before Excel tries to print to a printer.

- **Workbook_BeforeSave.** When you choose to save a workbook to disk, this event is triggered immediately before the file is written to the disk.

- **Workbook_BeforeXmlExport.** This event is triggered just before a workbook is saved in XML format or a workbook data is exported in XML format.

- **Workbook_BeforeXmlImport.** This event is triggered just before XML data is imported inot a workbook or just before an XML data connection is refreshed.

- **Workbook_Deactivate.** This event is triggered when the workbook is deactivated (something other than the workbook is selected or has focus).

- **Workbook_ModelChange.** This event is triggered when the user modifies the data model in some manner, such as adding or deleting columns and rows.

- **Workbook_NewChart.** This event is triggered whenever you add a new chart (either embedded or sheet-sized) to the workbook.

- **Workbook_NewSheet.** This event is triggered when you create a new worksheet in the workbook.

- **Workbook_Open.** This event occurs when the workbook is first opened within Excel; it is the opposite of the Workbook_BeforeClose event. This event is typically used to configure Excel in some way in prepraration for working on this particular workbook.

- **Workbook_PivotTableCloseConnection.** This event occurs when a PivotTable finishes grabbing source data and "closes" the connection with the source data.

- **Workbook_PivotTableOpenConnection.** This event occurs when a PivotTable gets ready to grab its source data.

- **Workbook_RowsetComplete.** This event is triggered when working with an OLAP cube and you complete work on a particular recordset.

- **Workbook_SheetActivate.** Every time a different worksheet is activated (selected) within the workbook, this event is triggered.

- **Workbook_SheetBeforeDelete.** This event is triggered just before a worksheet is deleted.

- **Workbook_SheetBeforeDoubleClick.** Double-click on a worksheet (usually the worksheet tab) and this event is triggered.

- **Workbook_SheetBeforeRightClick.** Right-click on a worksheet (usually the worksheet tab) and this event is triggered.

- **Workbook_SheetCalculate.** When you calculate a worksheet (either explicitly or by making a change that results in a modified calculation) this event is triggered.

- **Workbook_SheetChange.** This event is triggered whenever you change any information stored in a worksheet.

- **Workbook_SheetDeactivate.** When you select a worksheet, the previously selected worksheet is deactivated. That is when this event is triggered.

- **Workbook_SheetFollowHyperlink.** This event is triggered whenever any hyperlink, on any worksheet, is clicked.

- **Workbook_SheetLensGalleryRenderComplete.** This event is triggered when a callout gallery's icons have finished being rendered for a worksheet.

- **Workbook_SheetPivotTableAfterValueChange.** This event is triggered when a cell or range of cells in any PivotTable in the workbook are edited or recalculated.

- **Workbook_SheetPivotTableBeforeAllocateChanges.** This event is triggered before any PivotTable in the workbook is changed (updated) by Excel.

- **Workbook_SheetPivotTableBeforeCommitChanges.** When any PivotTable in the workbook is based upon an OLAP data source, this event is triggered just before changes are committed in that data.

- **Workbook_SheetPivotTableBeforeDiscardChanges.** This event is triggered just before changes to any PivotTable in the workbook are discarded (overwritten by new data).

- **Workbook_SheetPivotTableChangeSync.** This event is triggered whenever any PivotTable in the workbook is synchronized with a copy of data stored in a specialized Microsoft document server.

- **Workbook_SheetPivotTableUpdate.** This event occurs when any PivotTable in the workbook is updated.

- **Workbook_SheetSelectionChange.** This event is triggered every time the selection is changed on any worksheet in the workbook. (A selection is changed when someone changes which cells are selected in a worksheet.)

- **Workbook_SheetTableUpdate.** This event is triggered whenever a defined data table is updated.

- **Workbook_Sync.** This event is triggered when the workbook is synchronized with a copy of the workbook that resides on a specialized Microsoft document server.

- **Workbook_WindowActivate.** Each workbook is displayed in a window in Excel. When the window containing this workbook is activated, this event is triggered.

- **Workbook_WindowDeactivate.** Each workbook is displayed in a window in Excel. When the window containing this workbook is deactivated (a different window is selected), this event is triggered.

- **Workbook_WindowResize.** Each workbook is displayed in a window in Excel. When the window containing this workbook is changed in size, this event is triggered. It is not triggered if the application window (the window containing Excel itself) is resized; that is an application-level event.

The above list of workbook-level events is comprehensive for Excel 2013. This means that not all of the events shown may be available in earlier versions of Excel. (Microsoft periodically adds to the list of events and, once in a great while, deletes events.)

Most of the events for which you can create handlers are pretty advanced, having to do with things like remote servers, XML, and XML stores. In all likelihood, the only events for which you might create handlers are a handful of the events, such as the Workbook_Close, Workbook_NewSheet, Workbook_ BeforePrint, and Workbook_Open events.

Event Handlers and Worksheets

Excel also provides a set of event handlers that apply only to worksheets. There are a couple of ways that you can display the variety of event handlers available for worksheets, but this is the easiest method:

1. Create a brand new workbook, with nothing in it.

2. Right-click on one of the worksheet tabs at the bottom of the screen and choose View Code from the resulting Context menu. Excel displays the Visbual Basic Editor with a Code window visible for that worksheet.

3. Click the Object down-arrow and choose Worksheet.

4. Click the Procedure down-arrow to see the events that can be handled for the worksheet.

The Object and Procedure down-arrows mentioned in steps 3 and 4 are in the same position as indicated in Figure 3-4. When you perform step 4, you can see a number of various events. There aren't as many as there are for workbooks, but there are still a good number:

- **Worksheet_Activate.** This event is triggered whenever this particular worksheet is activated; in other words, when it is selected or "receives focus."

- **Worksheet_BeforeDelete.** This event is triggered just before the worksheet is deleted.

- **Worksheet_BeforeDoubleClick.** This event is triggered when someone double-clicks this worksheet or within this worksheet.

- **Worksheet_BeforeRightClick.** This event is triggered when someone right-clicks this worksheet or within this worksheet.

- **Worksheet_Calculate.** This event occurs right after this worksheet is calculated, either explicitly or automatically.

- **Worksheet_Change.** This event occurs when something in any cell of the worksheet is changed by the user. In other words, when a person edits a cell's contents or pastes something into a cell. It is not triggered if the change occurs as a result of recalculation. It is only triggered once if a change affects more than one cell.

- **Worksheet_Deactivate.** This event is triggered when you "click away" from this worksheet. In other words, it occurs when the current worksheet loses focus.

- **Worksheet_FollowHyperlink.** This event is triggered whenever any hyperlink on this particular worksheet is clicked.

- **Worksheet_LensGalleryRenderComplete.** This event is triggered when a callout gallery's icons have finished being rendered for the worksheet

- **Worksheet_PivotTableAfterValueChange.** This event is triggered when a cell or range of cells in a PivotTable on the current worksheet is edited or recalculated.

- **Worksheet_PivotTableBeforeAllocateChanges.** This event is triggered before a PivotTable on the current worksheet is changed (updated) by Excel.

- **Worksheet_PivotTableBeforeCommitChanges.** When a PivotTable on the current worksheet is based upon an OLAP data source, this event is triggered just before changes are committed in that data.

- **Worksheet_PivotTableBeforeDiscardChanges.** This event is triggered just before changes to a PivotTable on the current worksheet are discarded (overwritten by new data).

- **Worksheet_PivotTableChangeSync.** This event is triggered whenever a PivotTable on the current worksheet is synchronized with a copy of data stored in a specialized Microsoft document server.

- **Worksheet_PivotTableUpdate.** This event occurs when a PivotTable on the current worksheet is updated.

- **Worksheet_SelectionChange.** This event occurs whenever a new selection is made in the worksheet.

- **Worksheet_TableUpdate.** This event is triggered whenever a defined data table on the worksheet is updated.

As with the workbook-level event handlers, these worksheet-level events are for Excel 2013. This means that not all of the events may be applicable to other versions of Excel. Also, most of the events that Excel triggers at a worksheet level can be ignored. The usual ones you may work with are just a few, like Worksheet_Activate and Worksheet_Change. Even so, it is helpful for you to understand the events that Excel pays attention to so that you can see potential areas where you can modify Excel's behavior by creating your own event handlers.

Event Handlers and Charts

Besides workbooks and worksheets, Excel also provides a number of events that are associated with the Chart object. The easy way to discover what these events are is to follow these steps:

1. Create a chart and make sure it is a chart that occupies an entire sheet.
2. Right-click on the tab for the chart sheet and, from the resulting Context menu, choose View Code. Excel displays the Visual Basic Editor with a Code window visible for that chart sheet.
3. Click the Object down-arrow and choose Chart.
4. Click the Procedure down-arrow to see the events that can be handled for the chart.

The Object and Procedure down-arrows mentioned in steps 3 and 4 are in the same position as indicated in Figure 3-4. When you perform step 4, Excel displays a number of events pertinent to the Chart object:

*   **Chart_Activate.** When the chart receives focus, then this event is triggered.
*   **Chart_BeforeDoubleClick.** This event occurs when someone double-clicks on a chart.
*   **Chart_BeforeRightClick.** This event is triggered when someone right-clicks on a chart.
*   **Chart_Calculate.** Whenever a chart's data is changed as a result of recalculating, then Excel triggers this event.
*   **Chart_Deactivate.** When the chart loses focus, then this event is triggered.

- **Chart_MouseDown.** This event is triggered when the mouse is moved over the chart and clicked.

- **Chart_MouseMove.** This event occurs as the mouse is moved over the chart. It is repeatedly triggered each time the mouse is moved.

- **Chart_MouseUp.** This event is triggered when the mouse button is released.

- **Chart_Resize.** This event is triggered when the chart is resized, normally by using the sizing handles.

- **Chart_Select.** This event is triggered whenever an element within the chart is selected.

- **Chart_SeriesChange.** When a chart is updated and part of the update includes a change in the data series used in the chart, this event is triggered.

In all likelihood, you probably won't be using any of the event handlers for charts. You can; there is nothing preventing you from doing so. However, most of the event handlers are considered fairly advanced in their usage. Normally they are used when you want to modify the appearance of charts on-the-fly, so to speak.

Automatic Macros

Besides the event handlers described in the previous section, Excel includes a few names for macros that it considers special. These special names, when given to your macros, perform tasks without any intervention on your part. For instance, you can create a macro that Excel runs automatically whenever you open a workbook or activate a worksheet.

These special macros that automatically run at predefined times are identified by special names. Otherwise, there is nothing different between these macros and any other you may write. Here are the names you can give macros so that they run automatically.

- **Auto_Open.** A macro that possesses this name is run whenever you open the workbook that contains it.

- **Auto_Close.** A macro using this name is run whenever you close a workbook.

- **Auto_Activate.** A macro saved under this name is automatically run whenever a worksheet is activated (when you click on it so it has focus).

- **Auto_Deactivate.** This name for a macro means that it is run whenever a worksheet loses focus (you click on something else).

Why would you want to use these automatic macros? You might have some special tasks that need to be completed relative to a specific workbook. For example, let's say that you have an important workbook and when it is opened by someone you want to remind the user to save it regularly. An easy way to do that is to simply create an Auto_Open macro and save it in the important workbook. It could be very simple, like this:

```
Sub Auto_Open()
    sTemp = "This is an important workbook." & vbCrLf
    sTemp = sTemp & "Please make sure you save this workbook" & vbCrLf
    sTemp = sTemp & "every few minutes while you are editing."
    MsgBox sTemp
End Sub
```

Once you save the macro with the workbook, then the macro is in place. The next time the workbook is opened the user is shown a message box with your request.

You should note that the automatic macros are included in the latest versions of Excel VBA for backwards compatibility. If you are writing your own macros from scratch, you'll want to use the appropriate event handlers to accomplish the same tasks previously performed by the automatic macros. Here are the ones you should use:

- **Auto_Open.** Use the Workbook_Open event handler.

- **Auto_Close.** Use the Workbook_Close event handler.

- **Auto_Activate.** Use the Workbook_SheetActivate or Worksheet_Activate event handler, depending on whether you want the macro to run when any worksheet is activated or when a specific worksheet is activated.

- **Auto_Deactivate.** Use the Workbook_SheetDeactivate or Worksheet_Deactivate event handler, depending on whether you want the macro to run when any worksheet is deactivated or when a specific worksheet is deactivated.

4

Understanding the VBA Environment

Visual Basic for Applications offers a simple approach to programming macros that work within the framework offered by Excel. With VBA you can quickly and easily create macros that automate common tasks and make processing your workbooks and worksheets a snap.

In this chapter you discover more about the environment in which VBA macros are run. Specifically, you learn how to use the Visual Basic Editor and everything that it offers. By the end of the chapter you'll have the following under your belt:

- How to display the Visual Basic Editor
- All the pieces and parts of the editor environment
- How to get help in the editor
- Ways you can customize how the editor does its work
- Exiting the Visual Basic Editor

Displaying the Visual Basic Editor

You've probably gotten the idea by now that the Visual Basic Editor is intrinsic to working with Excel macros. (If you haven't gotten that idea, now would be a good time to get it.) Regardless of whether you record macros and later edit them or simply create your macros from scratch, working with the Visual Basic Editor is critical.

There are a few ways you can display the Visual Basic Editor. Any of these methods work:

- Display the Developer tab of the ribbon and click the Visual Basic tool in the Code group.
- Press **Alt+F11**.
- Display the Macros dialog box and use either the Edit or Create buttons.

Regardless of how you start the Visual Basic Editor, you'll soon see a screen similar to what you see in Figure 4-1.

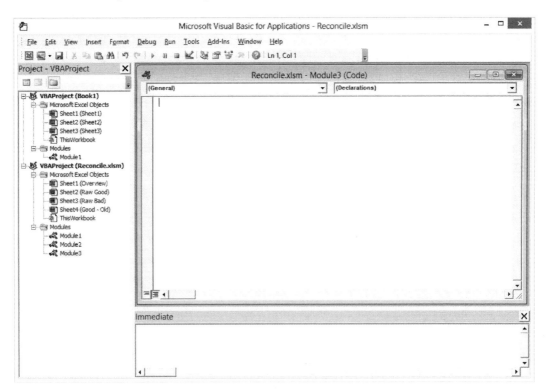

Figure 4-1. *The Visual Basic Editor is used to modify the programming code for your macros.*

The Visual Basic Editor uses the older, menu-based interface familiar to long-time Excel users. Don't worry if what you see in the Visual Basic Editor is a bit different than what you see in Figure 4-1; it is possible for some of the elements of the interface to be turned off or obscured by some other part.

Parts of the Environment

Throughout the earlier parts of this book I've essentially taken the Visual Basic Editor for granted, having you display it to accomplish some rudimentary tasks, but I never took the time to explain the different parts of the editor. Each part of the editor performs a valuable function, so you'll benefit by knowing more about them. The following sections examine each of those parts.

The Menu Bar

In order to get things done in the Visual Basic Editor, you need to learn how to use the menu bar. The menu bar contains the major categories of tasks you may want to accomplish with the editor. It is located just under the Visual Basic Editor's title bar:

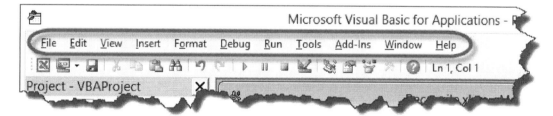

You can select menus with either the mouse or the keyboard. To select a menu with the mouse, just point to the menu name and click the left button. A pull-down menu appears. Using the keyboard, however, requires a little more information.

Notice that the first character of each menu name in the menu bar is underlined. The underlined character is the access key for that menu. In some other programs, these access keys are often called *hot keys*. To activate a menu, press and hold the ᴀʟᴛ key and then press the relative access key. For example, to pull down the File menu, press and hold the ᴀʟᴛ key and then press **F**.

After you pull down a menu, notice that each menu item also has an access key. Unlike the menu names, the access key for a menu item isn't always the first letter. This is because many menu items start with the same letters. If the first letter was always underlined, then the access keys wouldn't be unique. The access key would still work—Excel would simply cycle through all the menu items using that particular access key, highlighting each of them in turn. To execute a particular item, you would have to press the ᴇɴᴛᴇʀ key. For rapid access, reduced confusion, and ease of use, other letters in the menu item are defined as the access key instead. The underlined letter within a menu item is always the access key for that menu item.

Selecting a menu item using an access key is even easier than selecting a menu. Just press the access key without pressing the ᴀʟᴛ key. For example, to select the Save menu item, while the File menu is open, press **S** without using ᴀʟᴛ. What could be faster? Shortcut keys!

As their name implies, shortcut keys provide an even faster way of selecting menu items. Pull down the File menu again:

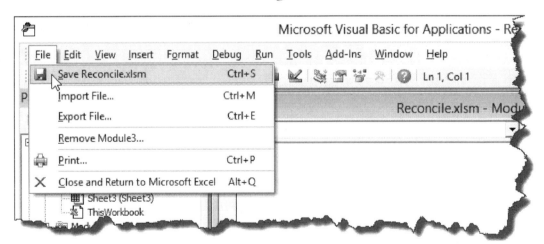

Notice the five menu items that have additional text on the right side of the menu list. For example, the Print menu item has ᴄᴛʀʟ+**P** next to it. This text represents the shortcut keystroke to access that menu item directly, without having to pull down the File menu and then select Print. The plus sign (+) between the two keys signifies that the first key should be pressed and held while the second key is pressed.

Try to access the same menu item using each technique. First use the access keys to select Print from the File menu. The Print dialog box appears. Then select the Cancel button to close the dialog box without taking any action. Now try the shortcut key. Without any menus pulled down, press and hold the CTRL key and then press the P key. The Print dialog box appears immediately.

While some shortcut keys are assigned for compatibility with other Windows programs (such as CTRL+P), the rest are assigned based on frequency of use. The operations performed most frequently are assigned to function keys. These are the special keys across the top or on the left side of your keyboard; each one begins with the letter F, as in F1, F2, F3, and so on. Operations assigned to function keys are handy because they only require a single key press. You'll appreciate this feature while you are getting started with the Visual Basic Editor. As an example, the very first function key, F1, instantly invokes the on-line help.

Some menu items are executed immediately while others require more information. A menu item followed by ellipsis points (…) indicates that choosing the item does not execute the command immediately. You'll either see another menu or a dialog box. You saw this earlier when you accessed the Print dialog box using File | Print.

While you are using the Visual Basic Editor, not all menu items are applicable at all times. When you can't use a menu item, it is grayed. Menu items normally appear as black text. When the text is gray you can still see the item, but you can't select it. Items are grayed rather than removed so you can remember menu item locations.

The Toolbar

The Toolbar is the row of picture buttons under the menu bar. The icons on the face of the buttons represent the action taken when you press that button. Each Toolbar button represents a frequently performed action.

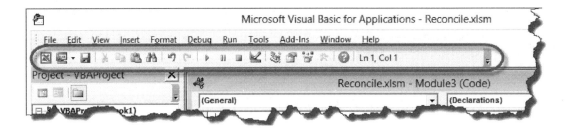

Using the Toolbar buttons makes performing actions faster and easier. Don't worry if you can't remember what each button does; there are menu items that perform the same operation as each Toolbar button. You can also get a hint as to what each Toolbar button does by hovering the mouse pointer over the button in question. After a second or two Excel displays a ToolTip that provides additional information.

If you look closely at the Toolbar, you may notice that some of the buttons lack color. For instance, in the above image of the Toolbar the fourth and fifth buttons from the left lack color. (These are the buttons that look like a pair of scissors and two sheets of paper. They represent the Cut and Copy commands, respectively.) If you see buttons that lack color, it means that they are "greyed out" and not accessible at the moment. Excel tries its best to make sure that only those tools that make sense at the moment are accessible.

You may find that you don't use the Toolbar and would prefer the additional screen space for other purposes. You can hide the Toolbar by selecting View | Toolbars | Standard. Notice that when the Toolbar is visible a check mark appears to the left of the menu item and when the Toolbar isn't visible there is no check mark. This is the editor's way of telling you whether the Toolbar is on or off.

The Project Explorer

VBA relies upon the concept of working with projects. Essentially, each workbook or template that is open in Excel is considered a project. These projects serve as "containers" (for lack of a better word) for groups of objects. In VBA these objects are things like code modules, forms, and references to objects in other projects. The different things that can be stored in a project were discussed in Chapter 2.

Helping you to keep track of the different projects open at any given time is the purpose of the Project Explorer. This window is visible, by default, at the left side of the Visual Basic Editor. If, for some reason, the Project Explorer is not visible on your system, you can display it by choosing View | Project Explorer or by pressing **CTRL+R**.

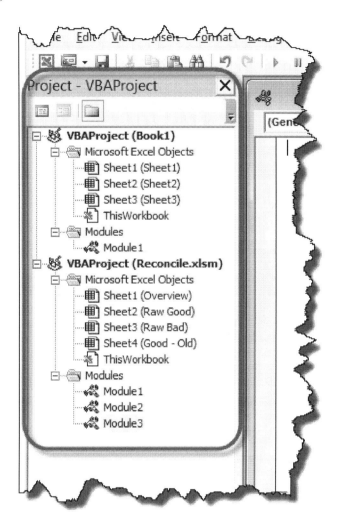

The Project Explorer is displayed in a hierarchical format. Notice that it contains textual descriptions of the various projects and their pieces, as well as a plus or minus sign to the left side of any item. The plus and minus signs are used to expand or contract each item, either showing or hiding the item's details.

The Properties Window

Another important part of the VBA environment is the Properties window. This window isn't shown by default, but it is easily displayed by choosing View | Properties Window or by pressing **F4**. The Properties window is used to display the behind-the-scenes properties for whatever you've selected in the Project Explorer.

In many cases—particularly if you are creating simple macros—you really don't need to worry about displaying the Properties window. (This may actually be the reason that Microsoft chooses not to display the window by default.) The Properties window is most valuable when your project includes user forms or other objects whose characteristics you want to easily modify.

There is a reciprocal relationship between an object in your project and the information in the Properties window. The information in the window changes as you select different objects or as you use the mouse to change an object. Conversely, you can modify the information in the Properties window and your changes are automatically reflected in the object.

If you don't have a specific need for the Properties window, it is a good idea to keep it hidden. You'll find that you have more room for other elements of the Visual Basic Editor (most notably the Code window) if you don't display the Properties window.

The Code Window

The place where you do the majority of your work in the Visual Basic Editor is known as the Code window. Because of its importance, the Code window typically occupies the largest portion of the Visual Basic Editor. The Code window is shown in Figure 4-2.

The Code window includes four distinct controls around the edges of the window:

- **Object List.** If your code module contains multiple objects (which is typically not the case), then you can select which object you want to work on using this drop-down list. When working on simple macros, the default selection of General is more than adequate. You

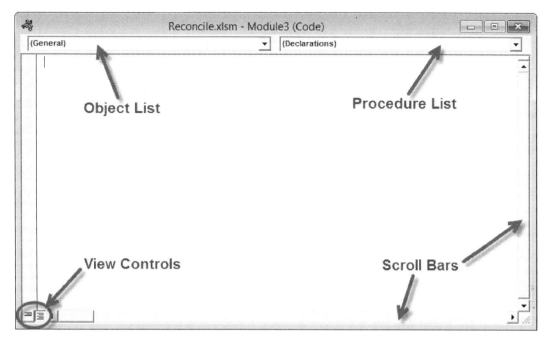

Figure 4-2. *The Code window is where you do most of your work in the Visual Basic Editor.*

also adjust what is shown in the object list if you are working with event handlers, as described in the Chapter 3.

- **Procedure List.** This drop-down list is used to specify the name of the procedure in which the insertion point is located. Generally it can be thought of as the procedure on which you are currently working. If you use the drop-down list to select a procedure, the insertion point jumps to the beginning of the procedure you choose.

- **View Controls.** The two view controls in the lower-left corner of the Code window are used to specify what is displayed in the window. The leftmost button, when chosen, displays only whatever procedure you are working on. The rightmost button, which is the default, causes all the procedures in the current object to be listed at once.

- **Scroll Bars.** These function just the same as scroll bars do when working with an Excel worksheet. They allow you to scroll left or right (the horizontal scroll bar) or up and down (the vertical scroll bar).

The Visual Basic Editor allows you to have more than one Code window open at a time in the editor. This comes in handy when you need to copy some of your programming code from one module to another or when you need to see how you accomplished something in a different module than the one on which you are working.

The Immediate Window

Just under the Code window is the Immediate window. This window may not always be visible, but it is a good idea to have it displayed as you are working with your macro code. This is particularly true if you are trying to debug your code, as discussed in Chapter 16. If the Immediate window is not visible, you can display it by choosing View | Immediate Window or by pressing CTRL+G.

The biggest use for the Immediate window is to try out some VBA statement or to see the value stored in a variable. I normally use the window while stepping through a macro. All I need to do is type, within the window, a question mark (VBA shorthand for "print") followed by a space and the name of the variable:

```
Immediate
? sTemp
Working on cell 34 of 525
```

You can also use the same technique to display the results of VBA statements or functions:

```
Immediate
? len(sTemp)
 25
? 2 + 4
 6
```

The Object Browser

The Visual Basic Editor includes a window that is normally not displayed. This window (and the tool it represents) provides a very valuable service. You'll remember from Chapter 2 that VBA allows you to work with what is called Excel's object model. When I introduced the object model, I demonstrated a way that you could discover information about the various objects within that model by using Excel's Help system.

Fortunately, the Visual Basic Editor also provides a way to access information about Excel's objects—through the use of the Object Browser. To display the Object Browser, choose View | Object Browser or just press **F2**. The Object Browser window pops into view, as shown in Figure 4-3.

To use the Object Browser, you simply pick an object at the left side of the window and Excel automatically displays the methods and properties applicable to that object at the right side of the window. When you find a property or method you want to work with, you can use the tools at the top of the Object Browser window to do the work. (I especially like the Copy to Clipboard tool, as I can then easily paste the property or method into my code or into the Immediate window.)

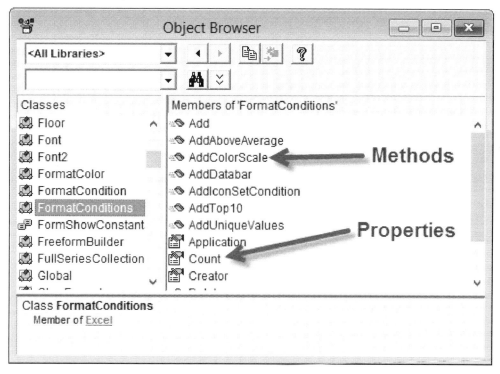

Figure 4-3. *The Object Browser window is helpful for discovering how to work with Excel's objects.*

Getting Help

The Visual Basic Editor comes with a complete on-line help system that is very useful as you learn to program. You access the on-line help system by any of the following means:

- Choose an option from the Help menu.
- Click the Help button on the Toolbar.
- Press the **F1** key.

When you choose the Help menu, another menu appears that lists the different types of help you can receive. These options are very similar to help options for other Windows programs; if you are comfortable with using the help system in other programs, you'll feel right at home here.

The other two ways to access the help system are essentially synonymous. The advantage of using either of these methods over using the menu is that they are context sensitive. This means that the Visual Basic Editor determines what you are currently doing and then displays the help information that it believes is the most appropriate to your needs.

For example, if you are typing a VBA statement in the Code window and you need assistance with a particular keyword, just make sure the insertion point is in the keyword and press **F1**. The help system springs into action and jumps directly to the information for that keyword. This method of accessing the help system also works for different elements of the VBA environment, such as the menu options, the Toolbar, and the Project Explorer. Just select the item that you need help with and then press **F1**. Figure 4-4 shows an example of the help screen displayed when you press **F1** after selecting the Project Explorer window.

Note that exactly what you see depends, in large part, on what version of Excel you are using. The screen in Figure 4-4 is what you see if you are using Excel 2013. If you are using Excel 2010, however, the help screen is quite different, as shown in Figure 4-5.

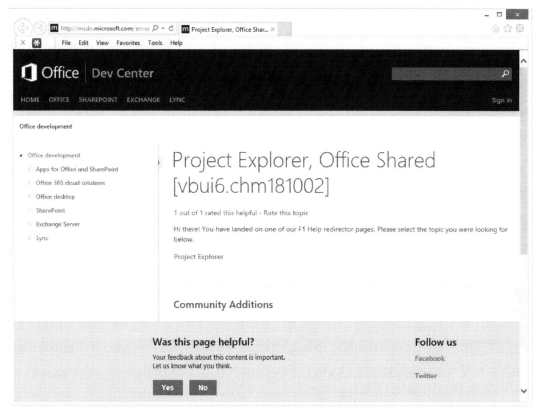

Figure 4-4. *The help system can provide context-sensitive help on a wide variety of topics.*

Searching for Help

One of the most powerful features of the help system is the ability to search for topics on which you need more information. The easiest way to do this is to display the help system window and then use the Search control. You can see this control in the upper-right corner of Figure 4-4 and just under the toolbar in Figure 4-5. (Actually, there are two Search controls visible in Figure 4-5. The top on searches the help system and the bottom one searchs the Web.)

Just type into the Search control the specific word or phrase with which you need help. When you press ENTER, the help system does its best to find something related to what you typed. It is a good idea to be as specific in your search term as you can. If you don't find any results with the first search, you can always alter the search so that it is more general in nature.

Figure 4-5. *The help system can vary dramatically from one version of Excel to another.*

Navigating the Help System

Take a look at a typical help system window, as shown in Figure 4-5. Notice that there are a group of buttons across the top of the window that allow you to navigate through the help file, reading information as you would in a book. In fact, the most helpful tool is the one that looks like a book. Click it and you'll see an outline at the left side of the help window. You can then use the outline to help explore the information available.

The Visual Basic Editor in Excel 2010 and earlier uses the standard Windows help system to display information. To fully describe all the features of the Windows help system would require an entire chapter in this book. It is a powerful tool that many VBA programmers come to depend on heavily while writing their programs. If you have never used the Windows help facility, you should take some time to explore it. When you need assistance, on-line help is usually the fastest way to get it.

If you are using the Visual Basic Editor in Excel 2013, then the help system is more Web-based, as shown in Figure 4-4. This means that you use traditional hyperlinks to move from topic to topic, choosing from those shown in the window. The handiest way to navigate the help system is to use the hierarchical Navigation bar at the left side of the window. Clicking options there allows you to "drill down" or move upwards through the available help options.

Customizing How VBA Works

Given the same office, no two individuals will organize it the same way. John may like his desk by the window and Jane may prefer hers facing the door. The Visual Basic Editor is so advanced that it allows you to customize virtually any aspect of the environment. Some of the changes you make may apply only to your current project, while other changes apply to all your projects.

Program Options

The Visual Basic Editor provides a great deal of flexibility that you can harness to control how the program works. For instance, some people may find that the default font used in the Code window is a bit too small for their taste. This—and many other program elements—can easily be changed as you desire.

To access these options, choose Options from the Tools menu. The Options dialog box is displayed, as shown in Figure 4-6.

Note that the Options dialog box includes four different tabs. Each of these contains a variety of options that you can modify, as you desire.

- **Editor.** This tab allows you to modify how the editor responds to what you type in the Code window. For the most part, you won't want to change anything here. The one possible exception is to enable the Require Variable Declaration check box. Doing so forces you to declare variables in your programs, which is always good programming practice.

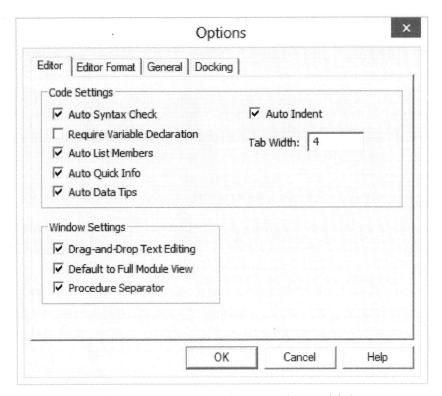

Figure 4-6. *The Options dialog box is used to modify how you work with the Visual Basic Editor.*

- **Editor Format.** This tab includes options that control the format of what you see in the Code window. Font size and color for various types of text are the primary options you can affect.

- **General.** Using the controls on this tab controls when the editor compiles the code you enter and what it should do if it detects errors.

- **Docking.** The various elements of the Visual Basic Editor, described earlier in this chapter, can be "docked" so that they cling to one of the sides of the program window. Docking is generally a good thing, but if you don't want some element to be dockable, you can control it on this tab.

The best thing to do is to remember that you can modify how the Visual Basic Editor does its work. As you become more familiar with the editor, you may want to modify various aspects of the environment to fit your desires. The first place to check for what can be checked is the Options dialog box.

Project Properties

Project properties are those options which affect the VBA project on which you are currently working. To change the options for the current project, choose the Project Properties option from the Tools menu. The Project Properties dialog box appears, as shown in Figure 4-7.

There are two tabs in the Project Properties dialog box—General and Protection. The first tab allows you to change the project name and provide a description for the project. It also allows you to associate a help file with the project and specify parameters that affect how your code is compiled by the editor. Most macro programmers don't really mess with anything on this tab; it is usually used by those who are writing full-blown VBA programs that are destined to operate as Excel add-ons.

The second tab, Protection, allows you to change parameters that affect who can see and change your programming code. For macros destined to be used solely on your computer system, this probably isn't necessary. It may be necessary, however, if you are creating macros that you place in a template for use by others in your organization.

Figure 4-7. The Project Properties dialog box allows you to modify elemental aspects of your VBA project.

Library References

In the Introduction to this book I mentioned that Excel is considered, by some, to be an extensible program. One evidence of this is readily evident in the VB Editor—you can specify which VBA libraries should be associated with whatever project you are working on.

A VBA library is a collection of functions and features that extend what you can do with VBA. By default, the Excel VB Editor comes with a default set of libraries enabled. You can, if you want, enable additional libraries or change which ones are active on your system. You do this by choosing the References option from the Tools menu. The References dialog box appears, as shown in Figure 4-8.

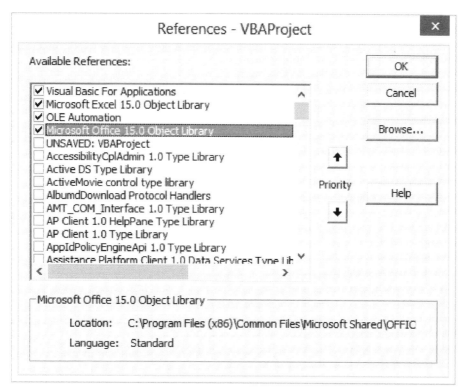

Figure 4-8. *The Referencces dialog box is used to control which libraries are associated with a project.*

Note that there are typically only a handful of libraries enabled for any given project, but Excel makes scores of libraries available. You should only need to change the library references if you have a specific need to access a feature contained within a library.

If you receive a macro from someone and try to run it on your system, it is possible that you might get an error that indicates a particular function is missing from the libraries. (The actual wording of such an error message varies widely and can, at first glance, be rightfully considered rather cryptic.) If you see such a message, you may need to do some detective work to find out what the offending function is and which library it is contained within. You can then use the References dialog box to enable the proper library and get rid of the error message.

Quitting the Visual Basic Editor

When you are done working in the Visual Basic Editor, you'll probably want to close it so that you can either quit Excel or start to work on a different workbook. There are three ways you can close the editor:

- Click the red Close button at the upper-right corner of the program window.
- Choose Close and Return to Microsoft Excel from the File menu.
- Press ALT+Q.

Any of these methods of quitting the Visual Basic Editor will do just fine. You may, however, want to make sure that you save your changes before leaving the editor. Most of the time this may not seem like a big deal. After all, your macro modules are stored in either workbooks or templates, so they are saved automatically when you later, in Excel, save the workbook or template on which you are working. However, I've known many people who wish they had explicitly saved their changes, in the Visual Basic Editor, when something unexpected happened in Excel that made saving impossible.

The typical way of saving your changes is to click the disk tool on the Visual Basic Editor Toolbar. This results in the saving of whatever project (workbook or template) is currently selected in the Project Explorer.

5

Managing Macros

When you start creating macros, it isn't long before you realize that you can use them for a wide range of purposes. Before you know it, you'll have dozens of macros that do everything from small tasks to major data processing. This presents a problem, however—what do you do with all those macros?

The answer is that you manage them and integrate them into your use of Excel so that they are easier than ever to use. This chapter covers some of the topics that can make you even more productive with your macros:

- How to add macros to the Excel interface
- How to create and change shortcut keys associated with macros
- Exporting and importing macro code

Adding Macros to Excel's Interface

You've probably come to the conclusion that Excel macros can be very handy to use. Done correctly, they can customize Excel to your specific needs, unlike virtually anything else you can do. It is not unusual for people to create an entire suite of macros that allow them to become more productive with Excel.

Because people use macros so often, it is not unusual for them to add the macros to Excel's interface. The following sections examine how you can make the changes for your macros.

Adding Macros to the Quick Access Toolbar

Excel is a very flexible program and a big part of that flexibility is due to macros. If you create a macro, you may want to add it to the Quick Access Toolbar so that you can quickly run it whenever you want. To add it, follow these steps:

1. Display the Excel Options dialog box. (In Excel 2007 click the Office button and then click Excel Options. In Excel 2010 or Excel 2013 display the File tab of the ribbon and then click Options.)

2. At the left side of the dialog box, click Customize (Excel 2007) or Quick Access Toolbar (Excel 2010 and Excel 2013).

3. Using the Choose Commands From drop-down list, choose Macros (see Figure 5-1).

4. In the list of available macros, select the one you want assigned to the Quick Access Toolbar.

5. Click the Add button. The command now appears at the right side of the dialog box.

6. Click the OK button. The command now appears on the Quick Access Toolbar.

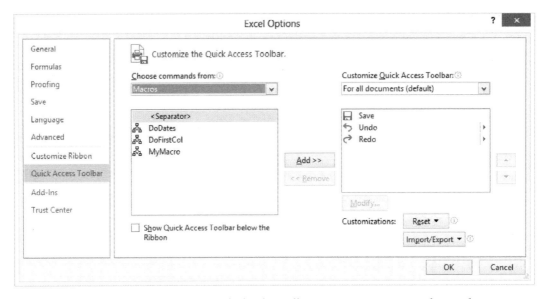

Figure 5-1. *The Excel Options dialog box allows you to customize what is shown on the Quick Access Toolbar.*

When you display the Excel Options dialog box, you may be surprised at the number of macros that are listed in the dialog box—there may be many more than the few shown in Figure 5-1. Remember that the macros don't only include those that you've created, but also any macros made available through any add-ins that you've loaded in Excel.

Note in the upper-right corner of the dialog box that, by default, Excel stores your customization so that it is available to all documents (workbooks) that you may open. If you want the customization to be available to only a single workbook or to a template, you can use the Customize Quick Access Toolbar drop-down list to specify your wishes.

In addition, you'll probably want to modify the icon that Excel uses on the Quick Access Toolbar for your macro. This is easy to do; all you need to do is click on the macro in the right column of the dialog box and then click the Modify button. Excel displays the Modify Button dialog box, shown in Figure 5-2.

Figure 5-2. *You can change the icon that Excel uses for your macro.*

Using the dialog box you can select from one of the many icons available for macros. When you click OK, Excel makes the assignment.

Adding Macros to Ribbon Tabs

If you are using Excel 2010 or Excel 2013 you can also add your macro to various tabs on the ribbon. This capability is not available in Excel 2007. (Actually, you can change the ribbon tools in Excel 2007, but the steps to do it involve quite a bit of XML gyrations and are beyond the level of this book.)

1. Display the File tab of the ribbon.

2. Click Options. Excel displays the Excel Options dialog box.

3. At the left side of the dialog box click Customize Ribbon.

4. Using the Choose Commands From drop-down list, choose Macros (see Figure 5-3).

5. At the right side of the dialog box, use the plus and minus icons to display the place on the ribbons where you want your macro to appear. Each item that possesses a plus or minus icon is considered a group.

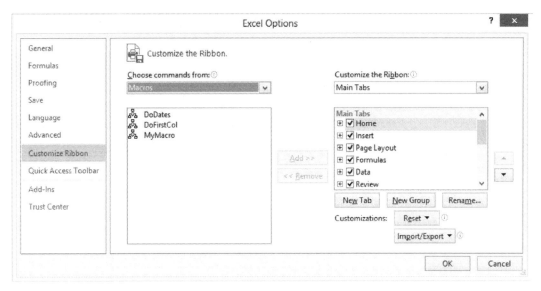

Figure 5-3. *Excel 2010 and 2013 users can add their macros to any of the tabs on the ribbon.*

6. Select the group after which you want your macro to appear.

7. Click the New Group button. Excel adds a group to the ribbon, right after the group you selected in step 6. This group is used to contain your macros. Note that the new group should now be selected.

8. Click the Rename button. Excel displays the Rename dialog box, which looks very similar to the Modify Button dialog box shown in Figure 5-2.

9. Modify the name of the group, as desired, in the Display Name box.

10. Click OK to close the Rename dialog box. Your new group should still be selected in the Excel Options dialog box.

11. In the list of available macros (left side of the dialog box) select the one you want added to your new group.

12. Click the Add button. The command now appears at the right side of the dialog box.

13. Click the OK button. The command now appears on the ribbon at the point where you added it.

Note that you can change the icon used for the command by using the Modify button after step 12, the same as described in the previous section.

Creating Shortcut Keys for Macros

Excel allows you to easily assign macros to specific key combinations. These key combinations are referred to as ***shortcut keys***, and they allow you to run the macro simply by using the shortcut key. When you first create a macro by recording it, Excel gives you the opportunity to assign the macro to a specific key combination. You do this by using the Shortcut Key setting in the Record Macro dialog box.

In my experience, most people don't assign a shortcut key to a macro right off the bat. Instead, they wait to make sure the macro is going to work and then they assign a shortcut key to the existing macro. Follow these steps:

1. Press **ALT+F8** to display the Macro dialog box, shown in Figure 5-4.

Figure 5-4. *The Macro dialog box lists all your macros in one place.*

2. From the list of available macros, select the macro whose shortcut key you want to change.

3. Click on Options. Excel displays the Macro Options dialog box.

4. In the Shortcut Key area, indicate the key you want used with the Cᴛʀʟ key as your shortcut. For instance, if you want Cᴛʀʟ+Y to execute your macro, then enter a **Y** in the Shortcut Key area.

5. Click on OK to close the Macro Options dialog box.

6. Click on Cancel to close the Macro dialog box.

If you later want to remove the association between the shortcut key and the macro, you can follow the same steps. The only exception is that in step 4 you'll remove any characters in the Shortcut Key area.

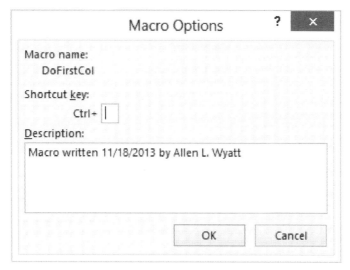

Figure 5-5. *You can assign a shortcut key to your macro*
so it can be run from the keyboard.

Exporting Macros

You already know that macros are stored in workbooks or in templates and that you use the Visual Basic Editor to make changes to the macros. One often overlooked feature of the editor, however, is the ability to export macros to their own file. The Visual Basic Editor allows you to export to a plain-text file, one that can be opened with any text editor, such as Notepad.

You can't export individual macros, but you can export entire modules of macros. (Remember that modules can contain a large number of macros.) You do it by following these steps:

1. Press ALT+F11 to display the Visual Basic Editor.

2. Use the Project Explorer to select the module you want to export.

3. Choose Export File from the File menu. Excel displays the Export File dialog box, shown in Figure 5-6.

4. Provide a filename for the export file. (Note that files should use the .Bas filename extension. This indicates that the file contains Visual Basic programming instructions.)

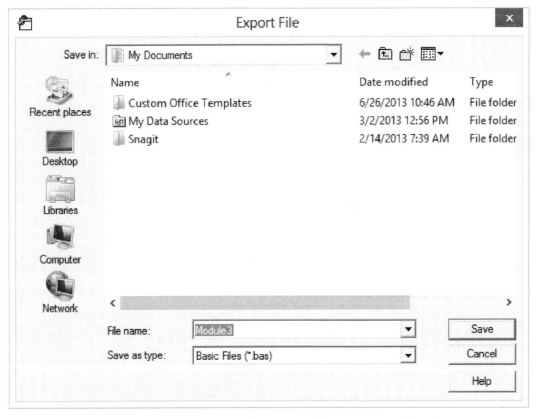

Figure 5-6. *Exporting a module to a text file is easy using the editor's Export File feature.*

5. Use the controls in the dialog box to select the folder in which you want the export file saved.

6. Click Save.

That's it; the module remains in the Visual Basic Editor, but now you also have a text file on your hard drive that contains the code. You can open the file with any text editor—just right-click on it and choose to open with Notepad.

It is a good idea to export macros if you want to easily move them from your system to an entirely different computer system. All you need to do is store the exported code in a place where you can access it from the other system, such as a network drive or a thumb drive. You can then follow the instructions in the next section to import the module to the other system.

If your module has quite a few macros in it and you only want a single macro out of the module, then exporting may be overkill. Instead you should consider simply copying the macro to a text file. You can do this by simply selecting the procedure in the Code window, pressing **CTRL+C** to copy it to the Clipboard, and then pasting the procedure into a text file you create in Notepad.

Importing Macros

Importing macros is the opposite of exporting them. If you want to import a module, you can do it by just following a few simple steps:

1. Press **ALT+F11** to display the Visual Basic Editor.

2. Use the Project Explorer to select the project into which you want the module imported.

3. Choose Import File from the File menu. Excel displays the Import File dialog box, which looks very much like a standard Open dialog box.

4. Use the controls in the dialog box to locate and select the module you want to import.

5. Click the Open dialog box.

The module is loaded from the file and attached to the project you specified in step 2.

You should note that you should only try to import modules you previously exported using the instructions in the previous section. If you try to import a module created in some other way, you may be at the mercy of how the Visual Basic Editor parses that file. If it contains errors, it can cause problems with the project that contains it.

6

Using Built-In Functions

VBA offers an extremely rich set of built-in functions for manipulating dates, times, strings, and numbers. Built-in functions are important because they save you time and effort—you don't need to reinvent the wheel.

In this chapter you discover how to use functions in your programs. You'll learn the syntax and nuances of various functions that can make your programming life easier. By the time you reach the end of this chapter, you'll know how functions are used.

Not all VBA functions are covered in this chapter. (There wouldn't be enough room!) Some of the functions that are not discussed in this chapter include financial calculations, advanced mathematical operations (such as transcendental functions), error-handling functions, and a bunch of miscellaneous functions. All the fundamental functions you need to develop most of your programs, however, are included.

The Benefits of Functions

It doesn't take much thought to recognize the benefits of using built-in functions. For example, imagine how long it would take to accomplish the seemingly simple task of determining whether today is Monday. You would have to figure out how to get the date from your PC, find a formula for calculating the day of the week given that date, and write a small program to implement it. But VBA's Weekday function returns the day of the week in one easy step.

To continue the example, if there weren't built-in functions for working with dates, you would have to buy or borrow reference material on PC internals in order to know where and how the date is stored. You would also need to figure out a way to access the specific memory location containing the date and time information—not an easy task since VBA has no inherent means of accessing a specific memory location. There are third-party tools to give you access to memory, but you would still need a formula to calculate the day of the week. Even if you already had these items, it would take at least an hour to write the program and test it. In contrast, it takes only a moment to find the built-in function you need and incorporate it in your program.

Date and Time Functions

How many days have passed since your birth? On what day of the week is Christmas next year? How long until your anniversary? When will your home mortgage be paid off? The answers to these questions require the ability to work with dates.

To determine how many days have passed since your birth, you must subtract your birth date from the current date. VBA has a function to calculate the difference between two dates, and you'll see an example of it later in this chapter. VBA also has functions that allow you to answer the other questions as well.

VBA's date functions work with dates ranging from before 1,900 years ago to about 7,000 years in the future.

Time is important to everyone on some scale. For a military operation, accuracy is often required to the second—or less; for a busy executive, every minute counts. Most people, however, are probably concerned with at least the hour. Even while on vacation you must stay conscious of the date and time, or you may be late returning to your more hectic life.

It's no wonder then that PCs keep track of both the date and time. VBA provides a variety of functions that allow you to access and manipulate both the date and time. Each function typically returns or uses the date and time stored in a variable using the Variant data type (see Chapter 2). This provides you with information you can readily use in your programs.

How VBA Stores Times and Dates

If you started a stopwatch at this moment and stopped it in 315,360,000 seconds how much older would you be? Because humans don't have the lightning-fast calculating speed of computers, it isn't very easy for us to make such calculations. With the aid of a calculator, you'll quickly see that you would be about 10 years older (not accounting for leap years).

What significant historical event occurred approximately 612,340 days ago? Again, most of us are at a loss. A properly programmed computer, however, would quickly determine the date as (again, approximately) sometime in May 337. With that information you can probably determine that it was the death of Flavius Valerius Aurelius Constantinus Augustus, commonly known as Constantine the Great, the 57th emperor of the Roman Empire. (For why that date is important, I'll let you do your own searching through the history books.)

VBA handles date ranges of this magnitude quite handily by storing dates and times as a serial number in a double-precision number. Everything to the left of the decimal point represents the date and everything to the right represents the time. You may remember from Chapter 2 that the range of numbers that can be stored in this data type is quite large; VBA can handle dates that cover about a 10,000 year range.

Determining Today's Date

The Date function is the starting point for many calculations involving dates. For instance, if you want to know how long ago a certain date was or how far in the future a certain date will be, you must start with today's date.

The format of the Date function is as follows:

```
Date
```

Pretty simple, huh? The value returned by the function is a Variant that can be stored in a variable in this manner:

```
Dim dTodaysDate As Date
dTodaysDate = Date
```

After this code is executed you can use dTodaysDate for any other calculations you desire or for displaying information to the screen.

Remember that when you use the Date function, the date returned is the date stored in the PC's internal clock. If the date stored in the PC is wrong, then the Date function obviously doesn't return the correct date.

Determining the Current Time

If you must know the current time of day, use the Time function. This is helpful if you need to record the starting time of some process you are about to perform or if you want to grab the time so you can add it to your worksheet. The use of the Time function is just as simple as the use of the Date function:

```
Dim dCurrentTime As Date
dCurrentTime = Time
```

Note that the value returned by the Time function is, again, a serial value. It is essentially a date serial number with the portion to the left of the decimal point set to 0. Because it is a date serial number you can store it in a variable that uses the Date data type.

Getting Both the Time and Date

Sometimes you need both today's date and the current time. You could use both the Date and Time functions, but there is a simpler way. You can use the Now function, which combines both Date and Time functions. Again, it is just as simple to use as both the Date and Time functions:

```
Dim dTimeDate As Date
dTimeAndDate = Now
```

Now is probably convenient for timing the execution of your program. To find out how long part of your program takes to execute, you could use code in the following manner:

```
Dim dStartTime As Date
Dim dTotalTime As Date
dStartTime = Now

    'code to be timed here

TotalTime = Now - StartTime
```

Make sure that the section you are timing doesn't contain anything that depends on user input (such as a button press or text entry) because it distorts the timing (unless of course, you want to time how long it takes for the user to respond).

Extracting Part of the Date

Sometimes you only need part of the date. For questions such as "Is today Wednesday?" and "Is this 2014?" VBA provides the following four functions for extracting only the part of the date in which you're interested:

- The Year function returns the year portion of the date. (The range could be 100 to 9999.)

- The Month function returns an integer from 1 to 12 (January to December).

- The Day function returns the day of the month (1 to 31).

- The Weekday function returns the day of the week represented by a number from 1 to 7 (Sunday to Saturday).

The format used by these functions is as follows:

```
Dim iThisYear As Integer
Dim iThisMonth As Integer
Dim iThisDay As Integer
Dim iDoW As Integer

iThisYear = Year(Date)
iThisMonth = Month(Now)
iThisDay = Day(Date)
iDoW = Weekday(Now)
```

After these code lines are executed iThisYear contains an integer value of the current year, such as 2014; iThisMonth contains an integer value of the current month, such as 12; iThisDay contains an integer value of the current day, such as 30; and iDoW is in the range 1 to 7, where 1 represents Sunday, 2 represents Monday, and so on through 7, which represents Saturday.

Displaying a Weekday Name

If someone asks you "When was the last time you used your PC?" would you answer "Last 3."? No, of course not. For calculation purposes, the integers returned by the Weekday function work just fine, but for display they just won't do. That's where the WeekdayName function comes into play.

```
Sub TypeWeekday()
    Dim iDoW As Integer

    iDoW = Weekday(Now)
    Range("A1").Value = WeekdayName(iDoW)
End Sub
```

Remember that the Weekday function returns a number of 1 through 7, which corresponds to Sunday through Saturday. The WeekdayName function takes that number and returns a full weekday name, such as Monday, Tuesday, etc. If you run this example, the macro places today's weekday name into cell A1.

Extracting Part of the Time

If you were only interested in a portion of the time (for example, the hour), you could use VBA's string functions to separate out the part in which you were interested.

Given the time 7:45:05 you could use InStr to find the first and second colon. Then, depending on which portion of the time you were interested in, you could use the Mid function to obtain that part. An easier way, however, is by using any of the following functions: Hour, Minute and Second.

```
Dim iThisHour As Integer
Dim iThisMinute As Integer
Dim iThisSecond As Integer
```

```
iThisHour = Hour(Now)
iThisMinute = Minute(Now)
iThisSecond = Second(Now)
```

When this example is executed, iThisHour contains an integer value of the current hour, from 0 and 23; iThisMinute contains an integer value of the current minute, between 0 and 59; and iThisSecond contains an integer value of the current second, also between 0 and 59.

Differences between Two Dates

Earlier in this chapter you learned that you could use one of VBA's built-in functions to determine the number of days since you were born. DateDiff is that function. The DateDiff function returns the number of days between two dates. If the first date is actually after the second, then DateDiff returns a negative number.

The format to use with this function is as follows:

```
DateDiff(interval, startdate, enddate)
```

Where *interval* is a string representing the units in which you want to measure the difference, *startdate* is the first date, and *enddate* is the second date. The *interval* value is specified as one of the following:

- yyyy (year)
- q (quarter)
- m (month)
- ww (week)
- y (day of year)
- w (weekday)
- d (day)
- h (hour)
- n (minute)
- s (second)

Remember that the *interval* must be expressed as a string, so here is one example of how you could use the function:

```
Dim NumDays As Variant

NumDays = DateDiff("d", Now, "6/5/86")
```

This example calculates the number of days since June 5, 1986.

Deriving a Date

To go the other way when you have a date and want to find a date in the future, it is best to use the DateAdd function. Its format is similar to the DateDiff function:

```
DateAdd(interval, number, date)
```

The *interval* is any of the same intervals that are used with the DateDiff function. The *number* parameter is how many of those units you want to add to the *date* parameter. Here's an example:

```
Dim dFutureDate As Date
Dim dPastDate As Date

dFutureDate = DateAdd("yyyy", 10, Now)
dPastDate = DateAdd("yyyy", -10, Now)
```

The first example sets dFutureDate to a date ten years in the future and the second example sets dPastDate to a date ten years in the past.

String Functions

You're going to start off the discussion of string functions with a short trip into the workings of your computer. Computers store all their information (even strings) as binary numbers. Binary means one of two states—either on or off, 1 or 0. Computers work in binary because the electronic switches of which they're made are only capable of storing a 1 or a 0 at any particular location.

The binary numbering system is also referred to as the *base two numbering system*. The value following the word *base* is the number of different values any one digit may have in that numbering system. In the decimal system (base 10), each digit can have a value from 0 to 9—that's ten possible values. In base two there are only two possible values—0 or 1.

To count in decimal, you start with a single digit. That digit contains the value 0. As you increment your count you increase the value in that first digit. When you reach the maximum value for that digit you reset it to 0 and increment the digit to the left. This process continues as long as necessary. Counting in base two follows the same rules, except there are fewer values to use in the digits. The first few binary numbers, corresponding to the decimal values 0 through 7, are as follows:

- 000
- 001
- 010
- 011
- 100
- 101
- 110
- 111

You can see how numbers could be stored using this system. But how does this relate to strings?

Characters are stored using a numeric code. By representing a character with a number, that number can be stored and later retrieved by the computer. When displayed, it is converted back into the character so that you can understand it. For instance, the numeric code for the capital letter *A* is 65 or, in base two, 1000001; for the lowercase letter *a* it is 97, or 1100001.

In order for computers made by different manufacturers to communicate with one another, a standard code was necessary for the representation of information. The first commonly used code for the interchange of computer information was ASCII (American Standard Code for Information Interchange). ASCII has codes only for the values 0 through 127. Windows (and thus VBA) understand ASCII, but they also understand more comprehensive coding systems that allow for the representation of many more characters.

Comparing Strings

VBA provides the StrComp function which allows you to quickly determine if two strings are equal. What about the following strings, however:

```
This is a test string
THIS IS A TEST STRING
```

If you use the normal comparison operators (Chapter 2) to do a comparison, these strings are not considered equal. With StrComp, however, you can instruct it to ignore the case of the letters in the string—it all depends on your needs. (If StrComp takes the case of the letters into account, it is considered *case-sensitive*.)

Here's how you use the StrComp function:

```
StrComp(string1, string2, [comparison type])
```

In this format *string1* and *string2* are the strings to compare and a *comparison type* of 0 performs a case-sensitive compare while a *comparison type* of 1 performs the comparison without regard to case. If the *comparison type* is omitted (remember that it is optional—that's what the [brackets] in the format example mean) then the normal default of 0 is used. The return values are:

- -1 if string1 < string2
- 0 if string1 = string2
- 1 if string1 > string2

Here's an example:

```
Dim iResult As Integer

iResult = StrComp("Test this", "TEST THIS", 1)
```

iResults contains a 0 because it was instructed to perform a case-insensitive comparison, so StrComp considers the strings equal to each other.

Converting Strings

More often than not, you'll need to make certain conversions in text strings used in your programs. For example, you may need to ensure that a last name contains an initial uppercase character or that a variable is stored in all uppercase so an exact match can be made. VBA's text conversion functions provide the means for easily manipulating strings.

Converting the Case of a String

For switching entire strings to all upper- or lowercase, the functions LCase and UCase work well. Pass the string to be converted to one of these functions, and a string is returned which is guaranteed to be all uppercase or lowercase (depending on which function is used).

To convert just a single character, separate that character, convert it, and then splice it back in. Listing 5.5 shows an example of capitalizing the initial letter of a word using UCase.

```
Dim sLower As String
Dim sProper As String

sLower = "herberger"
sProper = UCase(Left(sLower,1)) & Mid(sLower,2)
```

When this code is executed, the sProper variable contains the proper capitalization for the name: Herberger.

Converting Characters to Values

You can use the Asc function to convert a single character to its underlying numeric code. Asc returns an integer value which is the numeric value of first character in a string. Here's an example:

```
Dim iNumValue As Integer

iNumValue = Asc("C")
```

When this code is executed, iNumValue contains the value 67. If the string passed to the Asc function is longer than a single character then the function only pays attention to the first character of the string.

Converting Values to Characters

The Chr function does just the opposite of Asc—it converts a number into an actual character. It is just as easy to use as the Asc function, as well:

```
Dim sMyString As String

sMyString = Chr(67)
```

When this code is executed, sMyString contains the uppercase letter *C*.

Converting a String to a Number

There are times when you want to convert a string to a number. This comes in handy when you get input from a user in the form of a string, but you must convert it to a number to process it further.

The Val function converts the numbers in a string into a value. If the string contains any non-numeric characters, then only that portion of the string before the first non-numeric character is converted. Val also properly converts a negative sign or exponentiation sign.

Here's an example to show how it works:

```
Dim lNum As Long

lNum = Val("12345abcde")
```

When this code is executed, lNum contains the value 12345. Remember: The Val function stops its conversion at the first non-numeric character in the string.

Converting a Number to a String

Many times you'll want to convert a number to a string, which is the opposite of what you did with the Val function in the previous section. The Str function allows you to convert a number into a string, adding a sign placeholder at the beginning (a space if the number is positive or a minus sign if the number is negative). For example:

```
Dim iOrigNum As Integer
Dim sNumOut As String
```

```
iOrigNum = 9876
sNumOut = Str(iOrigNum)
```

When this code is executed, sNumOut contains the characters " 9876". Notice the leading space, which is a placeholder for a negative sign.

Creating Strings

Occasionally you'll need a string of characters that are all the same. For example, you may be printing a report and need a line of dashes across the page. There are many ways to generate a string of some number of a specific character, but two built-in VBA functions, Space and String, are the easiest.

For instance, suppose you need a string of dashes to add to cell A7 and you want this string to be 40 characters wide. The following code inserts the dashes in cell A7, as desired:

```
Sub InsertDashes()
    Dim sDashes As String

    sDashes = String(40,"-")
    Range("A7").Value = sDashes
End Sub
```

While you can pass a string containing more than one character, the String function uses only the first character of the string. For example, String(5, "ABC") returns "AAAAA" not "ABCABCABCABCABC".

Often the character you need is the space, so there is a special function just for generating strings comprised of only spaces—the Space function. The string you construct using Space is no different than the string you get using String with a space character. If you prefer, you can always use the String function and forget about Space. Here's an example of how to use it:

```
Dim sMySpaces As String

sMySpaces = Space(10)
```

This example returns a string consisting of 10 space characters.

Other String Functions

So far you have learned that VBA provides quite a few different string functions. You have not learned them all, however. VBA also provides other functions that allow you to do things like determine the length of a string, determine if one string is contained within another, and extract different parts of a string.

Finding the Length of a String

It is often critical to know the length of a string. For example, if you are processing a worksheet and you are stepping through each cell of that worksheet, you may need to know the length of whatever is in each cell to determine if some processing can take place. The way you figure out the length of a string is with the Len function. Here's a way it can be used:

```
Dim sTemp As String
Dim c As Range

For Each c in Selection
    sTemp = c.Value
    If Len(sTemp) > 0 Then
        ' Do some sort of processing here
    End If
Next c
```

This example steps through whatever cells are selected when the macro is executed, examining the length of each cell's contents. The part you want to focus on is the Len function, which checks the length of the sTemp string. If it is greater than 0 then the processing can occur. (Ranges and selections are discussed fully in Chapter 10.)

Strings within Strings

Another thing you may often need to do is to check to see if one string is contained within another string. For instance, you might want to know if a particular string contains the word "at". One way you can do this is using the InStr function, which returns a number indicating where in the string another string occurs. If it does not occur, then the function returns a 0.

Here is an example of using the InStr function:

```
Sub CheckString()
    Dim sMyString As String
    Dim iLocation As Integer
    Dim sResult As String

    sMyString = "Where is the cat found at?"
    iLocation = InStr(sMyString, " at")
    sResult = "Didn't find it"
    If iLocation > 0 Then
        sResult = "Found it at character " & iLocation
    End If
    MsgBox sResult
End Sub
```

Note that what is searched for in this use of the InStr function is the string " at", with a leading space. This is to make sure that it finds a word beginning with the letters *at;* it precludes finding a match in the word *cat*.

Extracting the Ends and Middle of a String

If you only require the leftmost or rightmost portions of a word, then the Left and Right functions are the most convenient. All you need to do is tell VBA how many characters to strip from the string. If you want to pull characters from the middle of a string then you use the Mid function, which also requires a beginning location.

```
Dim sMyString As String
Dim sLeftPart As String
Dim sRightPart As String
Dim sMiddlePart As String

sMyString = "This is my very long string"
sLeftPart = Left(sMyString, 9)
sRightPart = Right(sMyString, 11)
sMiddlePart = Mid(sMyString, 9, 7)
```

Run this code and you find out that sLeftPart contains "This is m", sRightPart contains "long string", and sMiddlePart contains "my very".

You should note that both the Left and Right function only need to know how many characters to pull from the original string, but the Mid function needs both a starting character location and the number of characters to pull. If you don't provide a number of characters with the Mid function, then it returns the rest of the original string.

Math Functions

Mathematics is an important part of everyday life. You do simple math hundreds of times each day. You buy things and count your change, you calculate the mileage your new car is getting, and many more things involving simple math.

Sometimes the math you must do is a little more complex. If you're buying a house, you'll need more advanced functions to determine your payments, given a particular interest rate, amount borrowed, and loan duration. If you are a scientist, engineer, or machinist, or you have one of many occupations which require the use of more advanced functions, you'll appreciate the power inherent in VBA's math functions.

If you think math is too difficult or you don't have a practical use for it, consider some of the examples you are about to see. Everyone uses math to make life easier, and VBA provides you with the functions to perform that math more quickly and accurately.

Extracting an Integer

If you are just interested in the portion of a number to the left of the decimal point, Int returns it for you. This is handy in some mathematical calculations where you need to make sure you are working with whole numbers. Here's a simple example:

```
Dim dblMyLong As Double
Dim iMyInteger As Integer

dblMyLong = 52.94387
iMyInteger = Int(dblMyLong)
```

When this code is executed, iMyInteger contains the value 52. What if you're interested in only the decimal portion? Simple. Just subtract the Int part from the original number. The decimal portion remains:

```
Dim dblMyLong As Double
Dim iMyInteger As Integer
Dim dblMyDecimal As Double

dblMyLong = 52.94387
iMyInteger = Int(dblMyLong)
dblMyDecimal = dblMyLong - iMyInteger
```

Generating Random Numbers

Have you ever played a computer game where the computer deals cards, throws dice, or spins a roulette wheel? Did you ever wonder how the random outcome of those events was simulated? Using VBA's Rnd function you can easily generate random events.

Before using the Rnd function, you must understand that the random numbers generated by VBA are not truly random. This is why you may hear them referred to as *pseudo-random numbers*. A complete discussion of random numbers and the theory behind generating them would require a book at least as large as this one.

So, if you build a game of chance based on the random number generator in VBA and then develop a system which consistently beats your game, don't take your life savings to Las Vegas or Atlantic City—their games generate far more random numbers.

Here's a simple use of the Rnd function:

```
Dim sngHelterSkelter As Single

sngHelterSkelter = Rnd
```

The number returned by Rnd is equal to or greater than 0 and less than 1. You can also include an optional parameter with Rnd which affects the results returned. If the optional value is less than 0 then Rnd returns the same random number every time it is invoked. If the optional value is 0 then Rnd returns the same number as the last time it was used. Finally, if the optional value is greater than 0 then Rnd returns the next random number in its sequence. If you want to use one of these optional values (most people don't), then simply put it in parentheses after the function:

```
sngHelterSkelter = Rnd(0)
```

Something to be aware of when using VBA's random number generator is that each time the program is run, under ordinary circumstances the same series of numbers are generated. To ensure a different set of numbers, use the Randomize statement.

Typically, Randomize would be issued when your program is started, although it doesn't hurt to issue it as many times as you like. Randomize reseeds the random number generator resulting in a different sequence of numbers each time your program is run.

```
Dim sngHelterSkelter As Single

Randomize
sngHelterSkelter = Rnd
```

To generate random integers within a specific range, use the following formula:

```
Int((biggest - smallest + 1) * Rnd + smallest)
```

Where biggest is the largest integer you want returned and smallest is the lowest integer you want. Thus, if you wanted a random number between 50 and 75 you would use either of the following:

```
Int((75 - 50 + 1) * Rnd + 50)
Int(26 * Rnd + 50)
```

Determining the Sign of a Number

When performing mathematical operations, it is sometimes necessary to know the sign of a number, or whether it is equal to zero. For example, before dividing a number by a variable, it is good to know whether that variable is equal to zero. If it is, then the result of the division is indeterminate and shouldn't be performed because an error would be generated in your program. If you are about to take an even root of a number, you most likely want to know if that number is negative.

The Sgn function determines whether a number is equal to, greater than, or less than zero all in one step. This is better than first testing the value to see if it is equal to zero and then testing to see if it was greater than zero or less than zero. The Sgn function is faster and more compact. One real purpose of the Sgn function is to determine whether a value is negative before textually formatting it.

```
Dim iMyValue As Integer
Dim sMyMessage As String
Dim iMySign As Integer
```

```
iMyValue = -3
iMySign = Sgn(iMyValue)
sMyMessage = "equal to zero"
If iMySign = 1 Then sMyMessage = "greater than zero"
If iMySign = -1 Then sMyMessage = "less than zero"
sMyMessage = Str(iMyValue) & " is " & sMyMessage
MsgBox sMyMessage
```

When this code is executed, iMySign contains -1 since the value being tested (iMyValue) is less than 0.

Positive Values

In some calculations, such as square roots, negative numbers are not acceptable (unless you are prepared to write special and highly complex routines for handling imaginary numbers—not an easy task in VBA). Sometimes the calculation can continue by ensuring the number is positive. You could test a number before using it and multiply it by -1 if it was negative, thereby changing its sign, but there is an easier way.

The guaranteed result of the Abs function is a positive number. This function returns the positive value of number. Thus, if number was originally negative, it is changed to positive. If number was positive, it remains unchanged.

```
Sub FindSquareRoot()
    Dim dblResult As Double
    Dim sRawInput As String
    Dim dblSource As Double

    sRawInput = InputBox("What number?")
    dblSource = Val(sRawInput)
    If dblSource <> 0 Then
        dblResult = Sqr(Abs(dblSource))
        MsgBox "The result is " & dblResult
    End If
End Sub
```

Using the Abs function within the square root function guarantees that an error won't occur if UnknownVariable is negative.

Formatting

Formatting refers to the way in which you alter the looks of the information your program presents. The Format function allows you to easily format values for output. For example, consider the number 3.14159265359. When formatted as currency, it is shown as $3.14. When formatted as a percent, it is displayed as 314.16%. When formatted as a medium time, it gives 03:23 a.m. Formatting puts the number in context.

The format of the Format function is as follows:

```
Format(expression[, fmt])
```

In this format *expression* is a numeric or string expression and *fmt* is any of a wide range of different formats that can be applied. (For information on available formats, see the on-line help system.) Here's a quick example of how you can use it:

```
Dim dblDividends As Double
Dim sOutput As String

dblDividends = 4423.7463
sOutput = Format(dblDividends, "Currency")
```

In this example, the formatted string $4,423.75 is stored in the sOutput string. VBA doesn't limit you to predefined formats in this manner. You can also create your own formats, a task that is not terribly hard, but is beyond the scope of this book. You can find more information about custom formatting codes for the Format function in the VBA online help.

7

Controlling Program Flow

The real strength of the computer is not in its number crunching ability as much as its ability to make decisions.

VBA steps through your macro code one line at a time. In this sense, VBA follows the path you pave through your code. Decisions based on the comparison of two or more items allow your program to follow one path or another. The potential to pick execution paths is really what makes computers useful. Without this capability, a computer would just be an overgrown hand-held calculator.

VBA provides many ways for you to control how a program is executed. This chapter explores these flow-control statements and explains where each is appropriate.

Conditional Execution

In Chapter 2 you learned about comparison operators and how to use them in a program. One of the most common places where they are used is in conditional statements. These are programming statements that affect program execution based on the outcome of some sort of logical comparison. These types of statements are very fundamental to any programming language, and VBA is no exception.

There are three types of conditional statements in VBA. They are the If...
Then statement, the Select Case structure, and the Switch clause. The following
sections explain each of these statements.

If ... Then

If the phone rings, answer it. If the dog barks, call me. If I have enough, I'll
buy lunch; otherwise, you can. We use a form of VBA's If...Then statement on
a daily basis. In common use, we just leave out all the words for a completely
formed If...Then clause, or we substitute other words with similar meaning.

Take a closer look at the sentences in the preceding paragraph. They are
rewritten here in a more structured manner:

```
If the phone rings Then
    answer the phone.

If the dog barks Then
    call me.

If I have enough money Then
    I'll pay for lunch
Else
    you pay for lunch.
```

These examples look very much like the VBA syntax for the If...Then statement
because making decisions in your macros is much like making the simple
decisions you make every day. For this reason, If...Then statements usually feel
very natural.

At its most simple form, the If...Then statement can be used on a single line,
as shown in these two examples:

```
Dim iAge As Integer
Dim sPerson As String

If iAge < 13 Then sPerson = "Child"
If (iAge > 13) And (iAge < 20) Then sPerson = "Teen"
```

Note that the If clause uses some sort of comparison that evaluates to either
True or False. You can include more than one comparison, as in the second
example, but it still must all evaluate to True or False.

For most people, the multi-line version of If...Then is what is used in macros.

```
Dim iAge As Integer
Dim sPerson As String

If iAge > 20 Then
    sPerson = "Adult"
    Beep
End If
```

Between the start of the If...Then structure and the final End If statement, you can have as many lines of programming code as you want. You can get even more complex by using the ElseIf and Else statements within the structure. Here's an example where the Else statement is used:

```
Dim sSex As String
Dim sType As String

If sSex = "F" Then
    sType = "Female"
Else
    sType = "Male"
End If
```

In this example, the statements between If and Else are executed if the comparison is True. If the comparison is not True, then the statements between Else and End If are executed.

The ElseIf statement allows additional comparisons to occur within the If... Then structure. Here's an example:

```
Dim sSex As String
Dim sType As String

If sSex = "F" Then
    sType = "Female"
ElseIf sSex = "M" Then
    sType = "Male"
Else
    sType = "Unknown"
End If
```

When used with the ElseIf...Then clause, the instructions between If and ElseIf are executed when the conditions following the If statement are True. If they are False, however, the conditions after the ElseIf statement are evaluated.

If the second condition evaluates True, the instructions between ElseIf and EndIf (or the next ElseIf) are executed. If the structure contains an Else clause (as it does in this example) then the statements between Else and End If are executed only if the result of the last ElseIf were False.

Formatting If ... Then Structures

You should perform only the simplest of tasks with an If...Then statement on a single line. It is easier to pick out the statements being executed if you use the multi-line form. Besides, your code often grows in complexity as you add functionality to your programs, ultimately requiring the use of the multi-line form anyway.

In the examples provided in the last section, notice the indentation of the instructions within the If...Then structure. This makes the code more readable. It also helps solve the problem of forgetting to put an End If at the end of the If clause. When the executed statements are indented, you can easily see if you have forgotten the End If.

Indentation is especially helpful with nested If clauses. You use a nested If clause when you must make multiple levels of decisions, as shown in this example:

```
If X < 25 Then
    If X\2 <> 0 Then
        If X\3 <> 0 Then
            MsgBox "X is prime."
        End If
    End If
End If
```

At first glance, this example doesn't seem to offer any advantage over the following example code:

```
If (X < 25) And (X\2 <> 0) And (X\3 <> 0) Then
    MsgBox "X is prime."
End If
```

There are advantages, however, in nesting the If...Then structures. For instance, consider the example shown here:

```
If X < 25 Then
    MsgBox "Likelihood X prime is 10/24"
    If X\2 <> 0 Then
        MsgBox "Likelihood X prime is now 10/13"
        If X\3 <> 0 Then
            MsgBox "X is prime."
        End If
    End If
End If
```

The nested If gives you the opportunity to do additional work between checking each condition.

Using Not With If...Then

The use of Not can sometimes make an If statement more readable. For example, consider the following simple code which checks to see if a variable contains a False value or not.

```
Dim bHome As Boolean

bHome = True

    ' statements

If bHome = False Then
    MsgBox "No one here!"
End If
```

You can make your code a bit more understandable and shorter if you use the Not operator in your If...Then structure:

```
Dim bHome As Boolean

bHome = True

    ' statements

If Not bHome Then
    MsgBox "No one here!"
End If
```

The code in both of these examples works the same because conditions in an If...Then structure always evaluate to True or False. The Not operator negates, or switches, the logical condition of an expression—thus, Not True equals

False and Not False equals True. If you plan the names of your variables and what they contain, your code can be much easier to read. Code that is easy to read allows you to concentrate on solving the problem at hand; it also is easier for others to understand.

Select Case

Many of the problems encountered while programming require long and often complicated If...Then statements. For example, the following code is required to determine which digit (1 to 5) a single digit number is. This code would be twice as long if checking for ten digits. It would be almost five times as long if checking for every character of the alphabet.

```
Dim iDigit As Integer
Dim sTemp As String

If iDigit = 1 Then
     sTemp= "One"
ElseIf iDigit = 2 Then
     sTemp= "Two"
ElseIf iDigit = 3 Then
     sTemp= "Three"
ElseIf iDigit = 4 Then
     sTemp= "Four"
ElseIf iDigit = 5 Then
     sTemp= "Five"
End If
```

One of the most convenient program flow constructs is the Select Case structure, which you can use to get rid of all those If...Then conditions. It is easy to use and provides a good solution to a wide variety of problems. Here's an example of the structure in action:

```
Dim iAge As Integer
Dim sPerson As String

iAge = 7

Select Case iAge
    Case Is < 13
         sPerson = "Child"
    Case Is < 20
         sPerson = "Teenager"
    Case Is >= 20
         sPerson = "Adult"
End Select
```

Note that the start of the Select Case structure includes something (in this case the iAge variable) that is tested in each Case statement within the structure. The expression that follows any Case statement can be in one of four forms:

- A numeric or string expression such as Val(iMyNum) or sFront.

- An explicit value such as 3 or True.

- A range of values by using the To keyword as in "A" To "Z" or 5 To 9.

- A conditional range of values by using the Is keyword such as Is < 0 or Is <> 0.

If the expression used in one of the Case statements matches the value of whatever is being tested in the Select Case statement, then the statements associated with that Case clause, and only the statements associated with that Case clause, are executed.

When using the Select Case statement, it is good practice to account for all anticipated cases with specific Case clauses and use the Case Else clause to flag an error if an unexpected value is encountered. If you use the Else clause to handle expected values, VBA processes any unexpected values possibly leading to erroneous results or unanticipated errors.

Switch

The Select Case statement allows only one test expression, and all the Cases must be related to that single test expression. Switch is different in that you can test different test expressions within the same function. You do this by simply defining a series of expressions to evaluate and what should be returned if the expression is True. The Switch statement allows you to define up to seven comparisons and values for those comparisons. Here's an example that uses five pairs:

```
Dim sLabel As String
Dim sOpVal As String
sLabel = "Operation is " & Switch(sOpVal = "+", "Addition", _
                          sOpVal = "-", "Subtraction", _
                          sOpVal = "*", "Multiplication", _
                          sOpVal = "/", "Division", _
                          True, "an Error")
```

When done, sLabel is equal to a value dependent on what is in the sOpVal variable. VBA evaluates the test expressions from left to right. When VBA encounters the first True expression, it doesn't evaluate any further.

Did you notice that the last condition in the Switch function example is always True? To catch any possible errors in expected values, place a statement at the end of the switch that always evaluates True.

Looping Structures

Besides conditional statements, VBA also includes several different types of structures, or constructs, which allow you to repeatedly execute segments of code as long as certain conditions are met. These types of constructs can add real power to your macros.

For looping structures, VBA provides the following:

- For loops
- For Each loops
- Do loops
- While loops

By effectively using these four types of constructs, you can create tight, concise code that still accomplishes a great deal of work. The following sections describe each of these constructs.

For Loop

The For loop is probably the control structure you'll use the most in your macros. It is a compact way to execute a set of instructions a certain number of times. You can use Do loop and a counter variable, but a For loop is more convenient. This example shows the simple way in which the For loop is used:

```
Dim sFull As String
Dim J As Integer

sFull = ""
```

```
For J = 1 To 10
    sFull = sFull & " " & Chr(64 + J)
Next J
```

The For loop is executed ten times, and each time through the loop the value of J (which is the loop counter) is equal to one of the values, 1 through 10. When this code has executed, sFull is equal to " A B C D E F G H I J".

It is entirely possible to omit the counter name after the Next keyword in a For loop. Try to resist the temptation to do this, however. Using the variable name helps to match the Next with its For when you have multiple or nested For loops.

Incrementing the Loop Counter

Within a For loop the statements are always executed before the loop counter is incremented. If the increment causes the loop counter value to exceed the ending value, then the loop is exited. Otherwise it is executed again.

While it is possible to modify the value of a loop counter in a For loop, it can make following the execution of code difficult. Try to structure your code so this isn't necessary.

The loop counter is incremented by 1 each time through the For loop, unless you specify a Step value. Specifying a negative Step value causes the loop counter to be decremented. Here's an example of counting backward through a For loop:

```
Dim sFull As String
Dim J As Integer

sFull = ""
For J = 10 To 5 Step -1
    sFull = sFull & Chr(64 + J)
Next J
```

When this code has completed execution, the sFull variable contains the string "JIHGFE".

The loop test is not actually for equality, which can lead to potential problems. The following code results in the message dialog box displaying the values 1,

4, 7, and 10. The values contained in J through the loop are 1, 4, 7, 10, and finally 13. The For loop compares 13 to the ending value of 12 and because 13 is larger than 12, the loop terminates. If a For loop required an exact match on the final pass, it can enter an endless loop where the condition necessary for its termination was never met.

```
Dim J As Integer

For J = 1 To 12 Step 3
    MsgBox J
Next J
```

With a positive Step value the loop terminates when the counter is greater than the end value. If the Step value is negative, then the loop terminates when the counter is less than the end count.

Nesting a For Loop

For loops can be nested. This has certain advantages over a single For loop. A great example is if you are accessing each cell in some data stored in a worksheet. The rows could easily be considered the outer loop and then each cell in that row would be handled by an inner loop. Here's an example:

```
Dim J As Integer
Dim K As Integer
Dim iNumRows As Integer
Dim iNumCols As Integer
Dim sChkTxt As String

iNumRows = 50
iNumCols = 20

'Loop to select each row
For J = 1 To iNumRows
    'Loop to select each cell in the current row
    For K = 1 To iNumCols
        'Select the cell to check
        sLocation = Chr(K+64) & J
        Range(sLocation).Select
        'Copy cell contents
        sChkTxt = ActiveCell.Value
        'If empty, add "N/A" text
        If sChkTxt = "" Then ActiveCell.Value = "N/A"
    Next K
Next J
```

The total number of times the statements in the inner loop of a nested For loop execute is equal to the product of all the individual For loop iterations. In this case the total number of iterations is equal to iNumRows (50) multiplied by iNumCols (20), for a total of 1,000 iterations.

For Each Loop

One special type of control structure is available because of the object-oriented nature of VBA. You learned in Chapter 2 that Excel makes objects and collections of objects available to your macro. The For Each loop provides an easy way to be able to step through each object within a collection of objects.

As an example, let's say you wanted to look through each cell in a selected range of cells. You might want to find cells in which there is a border set. The following macro does that:

```
Sub SearchForBorders()
    Dim c As Range
    Dim bFound As Boolean

    For Each c In Selection
        bFound = False
        If c.Borders(xlEdgeTop).LineStyle <> xlLineStyleNone _
          Then bFound = True
        If c.Borders(xlEdgeLeft).LineStyle <> xlLineStyleNone _
          Then bFound = True
        If c.Borders(xlEdgeBottom).LineStyle <> xlLineStyleNone _
          Then bFound = True
        If c.Borders(xlEdgeRight).LineStyle <> xlLineStyleNone _
          Then bFound = True

        If bFound Then
            c.Select
            Exit Sub
        End If
    Next c
End Sub
```

Run the macro and Excel examines each cell in whatever range is selected. It finds and selects the first cell that has any border set. The important point to understand here, however, is the use of the For Each loop that is the heart of this macro. Notice the structure of the loop—you specify a variable as a proxy for each element of the collection. In this case, the variable is c and the collection is all the cells in the selected range of cells. Each time through the loop c is set to a Range object (a cell) within the collection.

Do Loop

One of the most versatile control structures is the Do loop. It allows you to check a condition and then execute a block of code if that condition is met. If the condition isn't met, the block of code is skipped over.

Intrinsic to the Do loop are the While and Until clauses. They modify how the loop works, specifying whether the loop is executed *while* a comparison is true or *until* a comparison is true. Here's a simple example of the loop:

```
Dim J As Integer
Dim R As Integer

J = 0
R = 1
Do While J <= 10
    Range ("A" & R).Value = J
    J = J + 2
    R = R + 1
Loop
```

This example types the value of J into your worksheet, each value into its own cell in column A. The first time through the loop the value of J is 0, the second time 2, then 4, 6, 8, and finally 10. Once J is incremented to a value of 12, the comparison at the beginning of the loop evaluates as False and the block of code is no longer executed.

This same example could have also been written with the While keyword and comparison at the end of the loop, in this manner:

```
Dim J As Integer
Dim R As Integer

J = 0
R = 1
Do
    Range ("A" & R).Value = J
    J = J + 2
    R = R + 1
Loop While J <= 10
```

The First Time Through

Given any task utilizing a Do loop there are usually several ways to accomplish it. You can use any of these formats of the loop:

- Do While...Loop
- Do...Loop While
- Do Until...Loop
- Do...Loop Until

Most of the time, you can select the Do loop version that you are most comfortable with and that reads most smoothly to you. You must be aware of one problem, which is exemplified here:

```
Dim X As Integer
Dim Y As Integer
Dim iIncVal As Integer

Do
    MsgBox "X=" & Str(X) & "   Y=" & Str(Y)
    X = X + iIncVal
Loop While X < Y
```

This is a very simple program. If your intent in creating the loop is to print the message box only when X is less than Y, then your logic has failed you. This loop always executes at least once. Instead, use an alternate form of the Do loop:

```
Dim X As Integer
Dim Y As Integer
Dim iIncVal As Integer

Do While X < Y
    MsgBox "X=" & Str(X) & "   Y=" & Str(Y)
    X = X + iIncVal
Loop
```

In this case, the test is done before the loop is entered the first time, and it is never executed if the test fails (when X is less than Y).

Exiting a Loop

VBA includes a statement you can use in the middle of your Do loop: Exit Do. If you use an Exit Do in the inner Do loop of a nested set of Do loops, it returns control to the structure one level above. In the following example, when the Exit Do statement is encountered, the next line to be executed is the last Loop statement.

```
Dim sCharBuffer As String
Dim sThisChar As String

Do While Not EOF(FileHandle)
    Input #FileHandle, sCharBuffer
    Do While Len(sCharBuffer) > 0
        sThisChar = Left(sCharBuffer,1)
        sCharBuffer = Right(sCharBuffer, Len(sCharBuffer) - 1)
        If sThisChar = "X" Then
            MsgBox "Found an X in this line"
            Exit Do
        End If
    Loop
Loop
```

Notice the use of Not in the initial Do statement—again for readability. You must not overestimate the importance of making your code easy to follow. A good programmer's source code reads like a story.

Exit Do isn't the only statement you can use to exit a loop; you can also use the Exit For statement. While Exit Do is used with Do loops, you can probably figure out that Exit For is used with For loops. Both Exit Do and Exit For function similarly; the only difference is the type of loop in which each is used.

While Loops

If you must perform an action over and over until some condition is met, but you don't know how many times it must be done beforehand, you can use a While loop.

In execution, a While loop is identical to a Do While version of a Do loop, as described in the previous section. One advantage of a While loop, however, is that it is syntactically the same construct as is used in several other high-level languages. This makes it more comfortable to use for some people who are new to VBA. Here's a short example of the structure:

```
Dim sResponse As String

sGetResponse              'Get user input
While sResponse <> "Exit"
    ProcessRecord         'Call procedure to process it all
    GetResponse           'Call procedure to get more user input
Wend
```

You need to note that somewhere in your While loop you need to have a way to change the value of whatever you are testing in the loop. If you don't, then the test always return True and your code remains in an endless loop. In the example above, the GetResponse procedure, called from within the loop, provides a way for the value of sResponse to change.

GoTo

You may have heard many bad things about GoTo. In the early days of BASIC, before the more structured flow control statements you discovered earlier in this chapter were available, GoTo was the easiest way to control program flow. This led to unmanageable code, sometimes called ***spaghetti code*** because of its similarity to a plate full of snarled spaghetti.

While it has been proven that it is never necessary to use a GoTo statement, it is sometimes convenient to do so. If you don't go overboard with GoTos, their occasional use, in situations that are difficult to solve with other flow control constructs, is considered acceptable programming practice.

Any time you are about to use a GoTo statement, take a few moments to consider whether one of the other program flow constructs can do the job in a more readable fashion. While you may have a good grasp of the overall flow within your program while you are writing it, when you come back to it in a year it takes a while to remember what you were doing. Too many GoTos can make it take far longer.

You can use either a line number or a label with the GoTo statement. Line numbers hearken back to the distant past when BASIC programs required each line to have a line number. VBA doesn't require line numbers, however, so if you use a line number with the GoTo statement, it is treated just like any other label in your program.

Here's how you use the GoTo statement, in general:

```
Dim bStopNow As Boolean

bStopNow = False
. . .
If bStopNow Then Goto Finished
. . .
Finished:
End
```

When executed, if bStopNow is changed to True before the If statement is reached, then the GoTo statement transfers execution to the line right after the Finshed label. Note the use of the colon after the label; such colons are not necessary if you use line numbers instead.

8

Using Data Structures

Frequently, when dealing with information, there is a built-in relationship between certain pieces of that information. For example, a book has a title, an ISBN number, a page count, and an author. Each book has a corresponding value for each of these items. VBA has the capability of using data structures so you can better handle related information.

In this chapter, you learn about the following:

- Data arrays
- User-defined data types
- How to work with data structures

Understanding Arrays

One of the most fundamental data structures is the array. An array is simply an ordered collection of data. Take ten dimes and line them up on the top of a table—you now have an array of dimes. For reference purposes, you can just as easily refer to the first dime in the array or the seventh dime in the array. Arrays are just a way of organizing things that have something in common.

Arrays of related items are used frequently in VBA. The benefit of arrays is that they enable you to categorize items and concentrate only on the element of the array in which you are interested.

When you have an array of similar elements, such as the array of dimes, you have more than just an ordered collection. You know that most aspects of the dimes are identical. All dimes are made of metal and all dimes are of approximately the same diameter, weight, and thickness.

If you collect dimes in the random change you receive each day, there is one thing that is likely to vary from coin to coin—the date of minting. If you were interested in describing your collection of dimes, you may write a list as follows:

- 1979
- 1972
- 1994
- 1983
- 1993
- 1991
- 1988
- 1976
- 1959
- 1924

Each of these ten dates could be an element in an array about your dimes. Each member of the array indicates a different minting year for dimes.

Setting Up an Array

To allocate adequate memory to hold arrays, you must declare the array so that VBA knows how to handle it. One way you can declare the array is to use the Dim statement, as you've seen used quite often through this book. Dim tells VBA to set aside the right amount of space for the array.

Here's the full format for using the Dim statement for arrays:

```
Dim arrayname([lower To ]upper[, [lower To ]upper]...)[As type]
```

In this format *arrayname* is the name of the array, *lower* and *upper* are the lower and upper bounds, respectively, of that array dimension, and *type* is the VBA data type of the array member. For example, you might use either of these to designate your array for dimes:

```
Dim Dimes(101)
Dim Dimes(1 To 101) As Integer
```

Arrays can also be declared Global so they may be accessed in all procedures and modules of your project. The Global statement has the exact same format as the Dim statement. Thus, you'd simply replace Dim with Global in the above examples. Doing so not only declares the array, but also makes it so that the array is universally accessible in your project.

There is one more way in which you can declare an array. You may have an occasion to use an array within a procedure with the requirement that the contents of the array be retained between procedure calls. In other words, you don't want the array to be reinitialized each time you enter the procedure. In these cases, use the Static declaration.

Static is used in the place of Dim when declaring variables in order to retain the value of the declared variable between calls to the procedure. Each Static variable retains its value as long as the program is running.

Changing Arrays on the Fly

Because arrays can consume so much memory it is convenient to change the size of the array as required during run time.

Frequently, you don't know how many dimensions or elements you have until after your program is already running. In these cases, it is also necessary to change the size of the array at run time. The ReDim statement does just that. Here's how you use the statement:

```
ReDim [Preserve ]arrayname ([lower To ]upper[, [lower To ]upper]...)[As
type]
```

When using ReDim, *arrayname* is the name of the dynamic array, *lower* and *upper* are the lower and upper bounds, respectively, of that array dimension, and *type* is the data type of the array member.

ReDim reallocates storage space for a previously declared array. The optional Preserve clause causes ReDim to retain the values contained in the array prior to the issue of ReDim. Note that if you use Preserve, you can resize only the last array dimension.

ReDim is used to modify the bounds of an array. In effect, it allows you to dynamically change how your arrays are used while the program is running. You can't use it to change the data type for a variable. For a non-dynamic array, you must get rid of the original variable entirely, and then you are free to redimension the variable.

If you want to free the memory space allocated to a dynamic array, use Erase. When you use Erase, you can get rid of the variable altogether:

```
Erase dimes
```

Multidimensional Arrays

Sometimes there is more than one aspect, or dimension, to an array. In the dim example, if you look closely, you can also find another feature which varies— the letter on the face of the dime representing the mint at which the dime was made. You can add another column to your list of dime years showing the mint next to the year. You then have a multidimensional array.

Multidimensional arrays are especially useful because they allow you to track and manipulate more than one aspect of the item you have placed into an array. As an example of the usefulness of multidimensional arrays, some of the characteristics of a family have been arranged into an array. This array shows several aspects of each family member:

Name	Sex	Birthday	Age	Occupation
Sam	M	5/8	27	Teacher
Ginger	F	8/11	24	Engineer
Beth	F	12/24	21	Student
Casey	M	6/13	18	Student

To represent the family member array in VBA, you must first declare it. Declaring the array sets aside memory space to hold the array elements. You learned how to do this earlier in the chapter, but you cannot use the Dim statement (by itself) to define an array for your family. The different elements of the array are of different data types. For example, the Name, Sex, and Occupation elements would be strings, while the age and possibly the date element could be expressed as a number. In this case, traditional arrays are all but useless. Instead, you need to learn about user-defined data types.

Getting Information about an Array

Arrays are quite flexible. They can have any number of dimensions, up to whatever your system memory allows. Because arrays are so flexible, VBA provides a way to uncover their bounds. You use the LBound and UBound functions to return the smallest and largest subscript of any array dimension.

```
Dim iHighEnd As Integer
Dim iNumElements As Integer
Dim sRPMArray(99) As String
Dim sBones(499, 3) As String

iHighEnd = UBound(sRPMArray)
iNumElements = UBound(sBones, 2) - LBound(sBones, 2) + 1
```

Starting to Count

You normally start counting at one. Computers and computer languages are typically different, however. VBA starts all of its arrays, unless told otherwise, at zero. You don't have to use the zeroth element if you don't want to; if you do, however, it is available.

Unless you specifically need it, having a zeroth element in all dimensions of all arrays wastes memory. Use the Option Base statement to force VBA to start all array indices from 1 instead of 0, thereby saving valuable memory.

The amount of memory regained depends on the number of dimensions in your arrays. The total memory an array consumes is the product of the number of its dimensions, times the number of elements, multiplied by the number of bytes required for the data type of each element in the array. By reducing the number of elements by one (when you use Option Base 1), you reduce the amount of memory needed to hold the array by the number of dimensions in that array. If your application uses arrays with many dimensions or if it uses many arrays, the savings can be significant.

Using the Option Base statement is optional. If not used, VBA starts all arrays with an index value of 0. If you decide to use Option Base, it must be used in the Declarations section of the project; it must also be used before declaring any arrays. It just requires a simple statement:

```
Option Base 1
```

If an array is declared using the optional To keyword, the array bounds specified with To overrides the bounds set by Option Base. The optional To keyword in the Dim, Global, Static, and ReDim statements provides greater flexibility in the control of array bounds. Its use is recommended.

User-Defined Data Types

Although occasionally you may have related information, the data types often vary. You may, perhaps, want to store information on employees in an array. Each employee has a hire date (Date/Time type), a name (String), a wage rate (Currency), and a job class (Integer). How can you use an array to store this information when the data types vary?

To store the employee information, you must first create a user-defined data type so all elements of the array can be the same. A user-defined data type "packages" a collection of other data types into an "envelope", which can then be treated as though it were a standard VBA data type. Here's an example:

```
Type Employee
    Name As String
    HireDate As Variant
    Dependents(10, 5) As String
End Type
```

The Type statement may only appear in a general code module, and you must place the statement in the Declarations section of the code module. This placement ensures you can use the defined type throughout that module.

The Type statement specifies the name by which this data type will be known—Employee. To obtain the value of one of the variables contained in a user type, use the name of the user type variable and then the name of the specific element in that type, separated by a period. In this way working with user-defined data types is like working with objects:

```
Type Dogs
    Name As String
    Age As Integer
    Breed As String
End Type

Dim PoundDogs(100) As Dogs

PoundDogs(5).Name = "Spot"
PoundDogs(5).Age = 4
PoundDogs(5).Breed = "Scottie"
```

One of the areas where user-defined data types are used quite frequently is with file access, such as when you are working with random-access files. This use of user-defined data types for this purpose is covered in Chapter 15.

Dialog Boxes

The word *dialog* comes from the Greek and means to converse. Dialog boxes are windows that convey information to the user of a program and often allow that user to provide directions back to the computer.

A good example of a dialog box is what you see if you try to exit Excel without first saving the changes to your workbook—the dialog box shown in Figure 9-1 appears. Here you learn what happens next, and then you are given the opportunity to respond to the potential action.

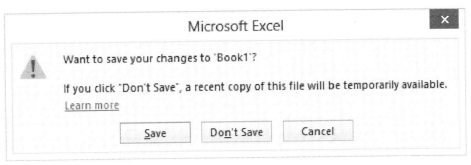

Figure 9-1. *Dialog boxes are used in Windows to communicate with users.*

Dialog boxes like these are an integral part of the Windows environment. You can make them a part of your programs as well. VBA provides several functions and facilities for adding and using dialog boxes in your programs. In this chapter, you learn about these capabilities and see examples of how they work.

Creating a Message Box

One of the most useful ways in which Windows programs have evolved in their communication with users is dialog boxes. Before Windows, dialog boxes were the exception rather than the rule. Even today programs written for many other operating systems often don't employ them.

The use of dialog boxes results in cleaner screens because the information to be conveyed or collected doesn't use up valuable space on your screen. You also can use dialog boxes to help guide a user through a specific problem and provide information at just the right moment.

In VBA you can create your own dialog boxes, as you'll see later in this chapter, but there is an even easier way—by using the MsgBox statement. The MsgBox statement is a flexible means of presenting dialog boxes in which you can change the message, title, and buttons shown; you can even add an optional icon.

The MsgBox statement probably isn't new to you. In fact, it has been used often in the various examples earlier in this book. The format of the statement is easy: You just follow MsgBox with up to three parameters. The first parameter is required; it is a string that indicates what message you want displayed in the message box. The second and third parameters are optional. The second is a numeric value that can indicate what buttons and icons should be displayed, and the third is a string that indicates what title should appear on the dialog box.

There are, in reality, fourth and fifth parameters that you could use. They are optional and aren't used very much at all. (They allow you to specify a help file for the message box and a context in which it operates—esoteric, indeed.) It is the first three that are the most often used, and it is these three that are examined in the following sections.

The Message

The easiest way to use MsgBox is in the form of a statement. All you basically need to do is provide a message you want displayed and VBA takes care of

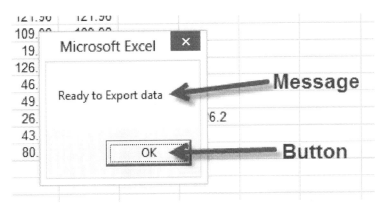

Figure 9-2. *A simple message box consists of a message and an OK button.*

the rest. The dialog box is displayed, along with an OK button for the user to click, as shown in Figure 9-2.

You can add a simple message box like this one to your own program—all it takes is a single statement like this:

```
MsgBox "Ready to Export Data"
```

Notice three things about this dialog box. First, the title that appears at the top of the dialog box is a default one that lets you know you are running this in Microsoft Excel. In the next section you'll discover how to change the title in the dialog box. Second, an OK button is shown in the dialog box, and your program is paused until the user clicks the button. This is the only type of button used for the statement form of MsgBox. How you can use different buttons is covered later in this chapter.

The message you used with the MsgBox statement appears in the message box exactly as you entered it. VBA adjusts the size of the dialog box to compensate for whatever text you enter, and it breaks lines as necessary. For example, consider this code:

```
Dim sTemp As String

sTemp = "This is the message for my custom dialog box and "
sTemp = sTemp & "it is much too long to fit all on one line. "
sTemp = sTemp & "Exactly how long it is depends on when I get "
sTemp = sTemp & "tired of typing. Are you tired of reading yet?"
MsgBox sTemp
```

Note that the code puts together a long message into the sTemp variable. When you run this code, the contents of the sTemp variable are used for the message in the dialog box. What you see is displayed in Figure 9-3.

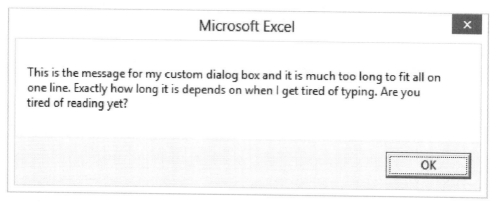

Figure 9-3. The MsgBox function can handle long messages by wrapping them to multiple lines.

Notice that VBA extended the width of the dialog box and wrapped the text to three lines. If you don't like how VBA splits the message over the additional lines, you can control it by adding the vbCrLf (carriage return/line feed) constant in your string where you want the message wrapped. An example of formatting the message in this manner is shown in the following:

```
Dim sTemp As String

sTemp = "This is the message for my custom" & vbCrLf
sTemp = sTemp & "dialog box and it is much too long" & vbCrLf
sTemp = sTemp & "to fit all on one line. Exactly how" & vbCrLf
sTemp = sTemp & "long it is depends on when I get" & vbCrLf
sTemp = sTemp & "tired of typing. Are you tired of" & vbCrLf
sTemp = sTemp & "reading yet?"
MsgBox sTemp
```

When the code is executed, the message in the dialog box (shown in Figure 9-4) is wrapped where you instructed. Notice, as well, that the overall width of the dialog box is narrower than when VBA controls the wrapping.

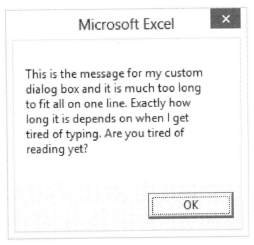

Figure 9-4. *You can control where the message in a MsgBox is wrapped.*

The Title

The MsgBox statement allows you to change the title of the dialog box as well as the message. You can make this change by simply adding another parameter to the statement, as shown in the following code:

```
MsgBox "Ready to Export Data",,"Super Exporter 2014"
```

The two commas separating the title from the message are essential. If they are not included, then you get a Type Mismatch error when you try to execute this statement. Normally, a value indicating a type of message box is added between the commas. These values are discussed more fully in the following section.

Icons, Buttons, and Responses

Much of the flexibility of the MsgBox statement is provided through the use of the second parameter. It determines which icons and buttons are shown in the dialog box.

149

Changing Icons

VBA allows you to use any of four different icons in your message boxes. These icons are rather standard for Windows dialog boxes; they seem to be used in virtually every program you can think of. You indicate an icon by using a numeric value for the second parameter. Here are the values you can use, along with their meanings:

- 16 or vbCritical (stop sign)
- 32 or vbQuestion (question mark)
- 48 or vbExclamation (exclamation mark)
- 64 or vbInformation ("i" for information)

Use the stop sign for serious errors or situations that can cause the loss of data. Use the question mark when obtaining answers to routine questions. The exclamation point is for situations that may have been unexpected by the user, or for emphasis of a message. Use the "i" when presenting a message purely for informational purposes.

As an example, try out the following program code:

```
Dim sMessage As String
Dim sTitle As String

sMessage = "You just eliminated the national debt."
sTitle = "Acme Problem Solver"
MsgBox sMessage, vbInformation, sTitle
```

When you run the code, you see a message box that looks like what you see in Figure 9-5.

Changing Buttons

Besides allowing you to add icons to your message boxes, VBA allows you to change which buttons are displayed at the bottom of the box. There are six different buttons that you can use:

- 0 or vbOKOnly (OK button)
- 1 or vbOKCancel (OK and Cancel buttons)

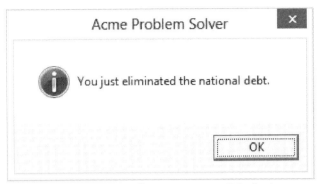

Figure 9-5. *VBA allows you to modify the icon displayed in a message box.*

- 2 or vbAbortRetryIgnore (Abort, Retry, and Ignore buttons)
- 3 or vbYesNoCancel (Yes, No, and Cancel buttons)
- 4 or vbYesNo (Yes and No buttons)
- 5 or vbRetryCancel (Retry and Cancel buttons)

Changing buttons in the dialog box is just as easy as adding icons. As an example, the following code would display a standard message box, but with Yes and No buttons at the bottom:

```
Dim sMessage As String
Dim sTitle As String

sMessage = "Do you want your program to work?"
sTitle = "Acme Program Fixer"
MsgBox sMessage, vbYesNo, sTitle
```

Combining Buttons and Icons

VBA allows you to combine both the icon type values and the button type values so that you can display both icons and different buttons in your dialog boxes. All you need to do is add the two values together.

For example, the value to display a stop sign icon is 16 (or vbCritical) and the value to display Yes, No, and Cancel buttons is 3 (or vbYesNoCancel). To display them both, you would use a type value of 16 + 3, or 19, in your program. Here's an example of how that works in your program code:

```
Dim sMessage As String
Dim sTitle As String

sMessage = "What should we do with the boss today?"
sTitle = "Company Relations"
MsgBox sMessage, vbQuestion+vbAbortRetryIgnore, sTitle
```

Note how the constants for the icon (vbQuestion) and the buttons (vbAbortRetryIgnore) are added together. The result is what is displayed in Figure 9-6.

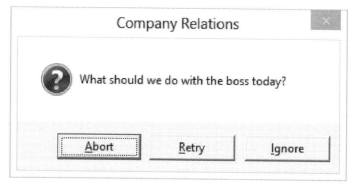

Figure 9-6. *You can combine icons and buttons in a single message box.*

User Feedback

It doesn't usually make sense to change the buttons being displayed in a message box if using them has no effect. So far you have done nothing but use the MsgBox statement, which simply displays the message box and then returns to your program. VBA provides a function version of MsgBox that allows you to determine which button the user selected. Based on this information, you can then take the appropriate action.

The biggest difference between using MsgBox as a statement and as a function is that when you are using it as a function, you enclose the parameters in parentheses. You also provide a variable into which the return value from the message box is stored. Here's an example:

```
Dim sMessage As String
Dim sTitle As String
Dim iYesNo As Integer
```

```
sMessage = "Do you want to proceed?"
sTitle = "Last Chance to Quit"
iYesNo = MsgBox(sMessage, vbQuestion+vbYesNo, sTitle)
```

You should note that the only difference between the MsgBox statement and function is that the function is used to return a value indicating which button the user pressed. After the MsgBox function has been invoked and the user has selected a button, the value returned ranges from 1 to 7, and corresponds to one of these seven possible buttons:

- 1 or vbOK (OK button was clicked)
- 2 or vbCancel (Cancel button was clicked)
- 3 or vbAbort (Abort button was clicked)
- 4 or vbRetry (Retry button was clicked)
- 5 or vbIgnore (Ignore button was clicked)
- 6 or vbYes (Yes button was clicked)
- 7 or vbNo (No button was clicked)

You can then make a determination of what to do based on the result. Many times programs use the Select Case construct (see Chapter 7) to take action after returning from a message box.

Getting User Input

A message box is great as long as you need only one of seven answers. What if you need more input? For example, what if you need to know a date to use when creating a new worksheet? When you need more input it is best to use the InputBox function. This function allows you to get a text string from the user and assign it to a variable.

The simplest use of the InputBox function is to specify a message you want to appear in the box, like this:

```
sRawInput = InputBox("Enter your name")
```

This results in a simple dialog box like what is shown in Figure 9-7. Note that the message is displayed near the top of the dialog box.

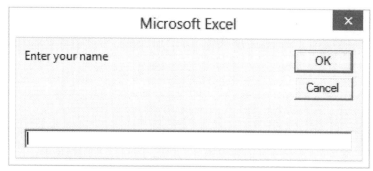

Figure 9-7. *An input box can be a very simple way to get user input.*

The InputBox function allows quite a few more parameters than just a prompt message, however. There are actually seven different parameters that are possible with the function, although it is only the first five that most people use. (The sixth and seventh parameters allow you to specify a help file for the input box and a context in which it operates. These are too advanced for the common uses of InputBox.) Each of the common InputBox parameters is examined in the following sections.

Remember that the InputBox function is designed to get input from the user. It contains only two buttons, as shown in Figure 9-7. If the OK button is clicked (or the ENTER key is pressed), then a string value of what was entered in the dialog box is returned. If the Cancel button is clicked (or the ESC key is pressed), then an empty string is returned.

The Prompt

As with MsgBox, whatever message you use with InputBox appears on-screen exactly as you type it. You are limited, however, to messages that are approximately 1024 characters long. Attempting to use a longer message results in a program error, but come on—if you can't get your message across in over a thousand characters, something may be wrong with your message!

If the message you enter is too long to fit on a single line, VBA wraps it automatically to the next line. If you want to make your message wrap at specific places, you can use the vbCrLf constant within the string, just as you can with the MsgBox statement.

The Title

Normally the InputBox function simply displays a title that lets you know you are working in Microsoft Excel (see Figure 9-7). You can, however, display a title more to your liking by adding another parameter to the input box function. Use the code shown in Listing 8.11 to generate a dialog box with a custom title and message, as shown in Figure 9-8.

```
Dim sMessage As String
Dim sTitle As String
Dim sRawInput As String

sMessage = "Enter the name you want to" & vbCrLf
sMessage = sMessage & "use for the new workbook."
sTitle = "Nifty Workbook Creator"
sRawInput = InputBox(sMessage, sTitle)
```

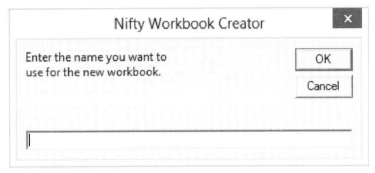

Figure 9-8. *You can specify a title for an input box.*

Default Input

By adding a third parameter to the InputBox function, VBA allows you to indicate default text that can be used in your input box. This text is displayed in the text box at the bottom of the dialog box, and the user can accept it by simply pressing ENTER or clicking OK. Conversely, if the user starts typing right away, the default is erased and replaced with whatever the user is typing.

As an example, the following code uses today's date as a default to the prompt. Note that the default should be a string value; in this case it is created using the Format function, as described in Chapter 6.

```
Dim sMessage As String
Dim sTitle As String
Dim sDefault As String
Dim sRawInput As String

sMessage = "What date do you want used for the worksheet?"
sTitle = "Nifty Worksheet Creator"
sDefault = Format(Now,"MM/DD/YYYY")
sRawInput = InputBox(sMessage, sTitle, sDefault)
```

Screen Coordinates

The fourth and fifth parameters that you can use with the InputBox function allow you to specify where, on the screen, the dialog box should be displayed. These parameters must be used as a pair; they designate the x and y coordinates of the upper-left corner of the input box.

You need to specify the position coordinates in a unit of measure known as *twips,* which are approximately 1/1440 of an inch. If specific screen coordinates are omitted, the dialog box is centered from left to right and appears about one-third down the screen from top to bottom.

Built-In Dialog Boxes

You probably noticed that Excel includes quite a few dialog boxes that spring into action at various times. These dialog boxes are the primary method that you use to configure how the program works or specify what you want it to do.

When it comes to VBA macros, Excel makes the vast majority of its dialog boxes available in the Dialogs collection. Since each dialog box is different, how you use them in your macro depends not only on what you want to do but on which dialog box you are working with. The following sections examine which dialog boxes are available and how you work with them.

Available Dialog Boxes

Excel uses dialog boxes—lots of dialog boxes. At last count, there were over 1,200 different dialog boxes that belong to the Dialogs collection. With that many dialog boxes, it can be hard to locate the one you want to use.

The easiest way to access a dialog box is simply to include its name within the parentheses of the collection, as shown here:

```
Application.Dialogs(xlDialogAlignment)
```

The problem is figuring out what names that Excel has assigned to the various dialog boxes. (This name is what you include in the parentheses.) With over 1,200 dialog boxes available, finding the names is no small task. Here's the easiest way to find them out:

1. Press **ALT+F11** to display the Visual Basic Editor.
2. Press **F2** to display the Object Browser.
3. Using the Project/Library drop-down list, choose Excel.
4. In the Classes list, choose <globals>. This should be the first option in the list. The Object Browser now appears as shown in Figure 9-9.

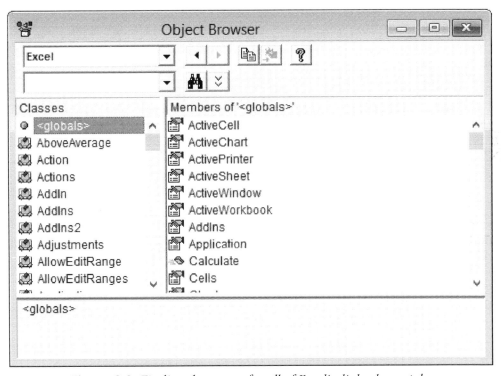

Figure 9-9. *Finding the names for all of Excel's dialog boxes takes a little sleuthing.*

5. Scroll through the Members of <globals> list until you locate the names for the dialog boxes.

The list of global names presented in the Object Browser is very long, but they aren't all names for dialog boxes. You'll know when you get to the appropriate names when you find those that begin with the characters *xlDialog*.

How Excel determines the dialog box name is rooted in history—it depends on the old (pre-Excel 2007) menu name and the command name on that menu. Thus, if you are looking for the dialog box that allows you to add a hyperlink to a worksheet, the proper name is xlDialogInsertHyperlink. The *xlDialog* is standard to all names, and *InsertHyperlink* refers to the old menu (Insert) and the command on that menu (Hyperlink).

If you prefer, you can find a list of Excel 2007 dialog box names at this address:

```
http://msdn.microsoft.com/en-us/library/bb240973(v=office.12).aspx
```

You can find a list of Excel 2010 dialog box names at this address:

```
http://msdn.microsoft.com/en-us/library/ff194519(v=office.14).aspx
```

Finally, you can find a list of Excel 2013 dialog box names at this address:

```
http://msdn.microsoft.com/en-us/library/ff194519(v=office.15).aspx
```

Displaying Dialog Boxes

Displaying a built-in dialog box is easy to do—all you need to do is use the Show method. For instance, if you want to display the Open dialog box, you could use the following code:

```
Application.Dialogs(xlDialogInsertHyperlink).Show
```

With the dialog box displayed, your macro waits for the user to take some action that results in the dialog box being closed. Once that is done, then your macro continues on its way.

Of course, you may not want your macro to continue blindly on its way after a dialog box is closed. Instead, you may want to get some feedback as to *how* the user closed the dialog box. This is done by checking what value is returned by the Show method. For instance, the following code is used to determine if the dialog box was closed by clicking Cancel:

```
Dim iRetVal As Integer

iRetVal = Application.Dialogs(xlDialogOpen).Show
If iRetVal = 0 Then
    MsgBox "You didn't pick a file!"
End If
```

The values that can be returned by the Show method are as follows:

- **-2**. The Close button was clicked.
- **-1**. The OK button or its equivalent (such as Open) was clicked.
- **0**. The Cancel button was clicked.
- **>0**. A command button where 1 is the first button, 2 is the second button, and so on.

If you want to take actions based on what button was clicked in a dialog box, you'll need to play around a bit and do some testing to see what is returned by the particular dialog box you are working with.

10

Working with Ranges and Selections

When working with pieces and parts of your data, the two most common objects you'll work with are either ranges or selections. A *range* is an object in Excel that represents, well, a range of cells. A Range object can be as small as a single cell or as many as 17,179,869,184 cells (all the cells in an entire worksheet).

A *selection* is most easily thought of as a range that has been selected—it is the selected portion of a worksheet. Macros you create often do their work using a range of cells that the user selected before running the macro, but you can also create a selection within the macro itself.

You can work with both ranges and selections within your macros, and you will often do so. Perhaps the biggest difference between ranges and selections is that there can only be a single Selection object in a given window, whereas there can be multiple Range objects defined. This means that ranges are much more flexible and important to your programming efforts.

With very few exceptions, you use the exact same techniques to create and work with both selections and ranges. The majority of this chapter uses references that apply to ranges, but they could just as easily apply to selections.

Because of how important both ranges and selections are to your macros, you'll want to pay particular attention to the information in this chapter.

Creating a Range

A Range object is a collection of cells that you define. The normal way to create a range is to simply specify the addresses of the cells you want in the range. For instance, the following code creates a Range object (StartCell) as equivalent to cell B7:

```
Dim StartCell As Range

Set StartCell = Range("B7")
```

If you prefer, you could specify a number of cells, in this manner:

```
Dim ManyCells As Range

Set ManyCells = Range("C4:J27")
```

The result is that the ManyCells variable now refers to the 192 cells in the worksheet range C4:J27.

Since Range objects can refer to any number of cells, it makes them very versatile and they can quickly become the workhorses of your worksheet processing.

It helps to think of a Range as a defined portion of your worksheet. When you create a Range object, you specify the part of the worksheet to which it refers. You can then use the Range in other operations, making it easier to reference that element. How you define and use the Range object is entirely up to you.

Creating a Selection

When you create small macros, the Selection object is typically whatever was selected by the user before a macro was executed. This is common, as it allows your macro to take its actions using whatever the user selected. There are times, however, when you may want your macro to actually create a selection and then take some action on that selection.

There are any number of ways you can select cells, depending on what you want to do. Excel allows you to explicitly select cells or to select cells that are relative to your current location in a worksheet. The various methods of selecting cells are covered in the following sections.

Selecting a Specific Cell or Range of Cells

The basic way that you create a selection is by specifying a range and then using the Select method with that range. For instance, if you want to select cell F3, you could use the following:

```
Range("F3").Select
```

Similarly, if you wanted to select the range of D4:Q7, you'd use this:

```
Range("D4:Q7").Select
```

The selection methods shown so far are applicable when you want to select cells in the current worksheet. If you want to select cells in a different worksheet, then you need to make sure that you select the worksheet just before selecting the cell:

```
Sheets("Sheet3").Select
Range("A18").Select
```

Interestingly enough, Excel doesn't allow you to condense the programming statement to a single line:

```
Sheets("Sheet3").Range("A18").Select
```

If you try, you'll end up with an error; the selection must be performed on two separate lines. Things get a little more complex when the cell you want to select is in a different workbook than the one in which you are currently working. For instance, consider the following two lines of code:

```
Workbooks("pwd.xlsx").Sheets("Sheet3").Select
Range("A18").Select
```

You might think that this macro will select Sheet3!A18 in the pwd.xlsx workbook. It does, with some caveats. If you have more than one workbook open, this macro results in an error, if pwd.xlsx isn't the currently active workbook. This occurs even if pwd.xlsx is already open, but simply not selected.

The only solution in this case is to entirely change how you perform the selection. Instead of using the Select method, use the Goto method and specify a target address for the method:

```
Application.Goto Reference:=Workbooks("pwd.xlsx").Sheets("Sheet3").[A18]
```

Selecting a Cell in the Current Row

If you are using Excel and you press the **HOME** key, the cell at the left side of the current row is selected. How do you perform the same action in a macro, however? Unfortunately, using the macro recorder to record this does not help, since it records the destination of the action, instead of your actual action. For instance, if you press **HOME** and you are on the fourth row in a worksheet, Excel doesn't record the Home action, but instead records the destination, as follows:

```
Range("A4").Select
```

This is great if you always want to go to cell A4, but terrible if you want to go to the first cell of whatever row you are on.

As with many tasks in VBA, there are several ways you can approach a solution to this dilemma. The first method is actually a variation on what the macro recorder returns, as shown above. All you need to do is change the row designator so it represents the current row, as in the following:

```
Range("A" & (ActiveCell.Row)).Select
```

VBA figures out what the current row is (by using the Row property of the ActiveCell object), slaps it together with the "A" designator, and comes up with a cell reference that works with the Range method.

The ActiveCell object is an interesting shortcut that is used to refer to whatever cell is currently active in the worksheet. Another technique relies on the ActiveCell object again, this time with the Cells function:

```
Cells(Application.ActiveCell.Row, 1).Select
```

The Cells function returns an object that represents a specific row and column (individual cell) of a worksheet. This approach, of course, can be modified so that you actually select any given cell in the current row. All you need to do is change the column designation (1, in the above example) to a number representing the column desired.

Another approach (which produces the same result) is to use the Range object in conjunction with the Cells function, as shown here:

```
Range(Cells(Selection.Row, 1).Address).Select
```

Selection.Row gives the row number of the current selection. The Address property of the Cells function returns the address of a particular cell in A1 format. This address is then used as the parameter for the Range object, and the actual cell is selected by the Select method.

Selecting a Range of Cells Relative to the Current Cell

In the previous section you discovered how you can use the Cells function to select a cell relative to the current cell. You can also use the same function to select a range of cells, as shown here:

```
Range(Cells(Selection.Row, 1), Cells(Selection.Row, 3)).Select
```

In this usage, Cells is used twice to determine a specific range of cells. The first instance returns the first cell of the current row, while the second returns the third cell of the current row. Thus, the range becomes the first through third cells of the current row.

Instead of using Cells to specify a location, a more flexible approach is to use the Offset property. Consider the following code:

```
ActiveCell.Offset(2, 1).Select
```

This uses the Offset property of the ActiveCell object to specify a range relative to the currently selected cell. The Offset property takes an argument that represents the row and column of the offset. A negative value represents up (for the row) and left (for the column). A positive value is down (for the row) and right (for the column). You can also use a value of 0, which represents the current row or column.

If you want to select a larger range than just a single cell, you can use Offset to specify the range you want to select:

```
Range(ActiveCell.Offset(-3, 5), ActiveCell.Offset(0, 10)).Select
```

In this case, the range that is selected begins three rows up and five columns to the right of the active cell and ends on the current row, but ten columns to the right of the active cell.

You can also combine the Offset method with the Address property to find actual cell addresses, and then use your findings to actually select the range itself. For instance, you might want to select the range that begins two rows down and one column to the right, but then extends for four rows and three columns. You can accomplish this in the following manner:

```
StartCell = ActiveCell.Offset(2, 1).Address
EndCell = ActiveCell.Offset(5, 3).Address
Range(StartCell, EndCell).Select
```

Working with Rows and Columns

Sometimes you'll want to work with entire rows of columns in your worksheet. This is easy to do using several different properties provided by Excel. Let's say, for instance, that you want to select the entire row in which the active cell is located. You could use this code:

```
ActiveCell.EntireRow.Select
```

Similarly, you could use the EntireColumn property in the above example, and Excel would dutifully select the entire column in which the active cell is located.

If you desire, you can also step through the rows or columns in a range of selection. Excel maintains a collection of rows and columns that reference the rows and columns in the original range. Oddly enough, these collections are called, respectively, Rows and Columns. Here's how you access these collections:

```
Dim rng As Range
Dim r As Range
```

```
Set rng = Range("F10:J15")
For Each r In rng.Rows
    r.Select
Next r
```

In this case it is the Rows collection that is being accessed, but it could just as easily be the Columns collection. When the Select statement is executed, an entire row of the rng object is selected. In other words, the first time through the loop the range of F10:J10 is selected, the second time through F11:J11 is selected, and so on, right up to F15:J15.

Editing Information

Editing a range or a selection is a simple task. All you basically need to do is make sure that your Range object is defined (the Selection object is always defined) and then start adding information. How you add the information depends upon how many cells are contained within the range or selection. The following sections demonstrate the editing techniques you can use.

Adding Values

Inserting values into cells is easy using a Range object. If your range points to a single cell, then you simply use the Value property to do the insertion. (The Value property, applied to a single cell, represents the contents of that cell.) For instance, the following code inserts text into a cell:

```
Dim SingleCell As Range

Set SingleCell = Range("B3")
SingleCell.Value = "My Inserted Text"
```

You could, of course, compress all of these lines to a single line, as in the following:

```
Range("B3").Value = "My Inserted Text"
```

The benefit of assigning the Range object to a variable, however, is that it makes it easier to work with a larger number of cells. Consider the following example:

```
Dim ManyCells As Range
Dim c As Range
Dim J As Integer

Set ManyCells = Range("C4:J27")
J = 1

For Each c In ManyCells
    c.Value = J
    J = J + 1
Next c
```

With a simple loop, each cell in the range is stepped through and a value assigned to it. This ability to set cell values is very powerful, indeed.

You add values to the cells in a Selection in the same way. All you need to do is instruct VBA that you want to work with the Selection object rather than the Range object, in this manner:

```
Dim c As Range
Dim J As Integer

J = 1

For Each c In Selection
    c.Value = J
    J = J + 1
Next c
```

This approach allows you to easily add the values to the worksheet and is particularly powerful when the user selects cells prior to running the macro.

Replacing Values

Using the information you learned in the previous section, you can easily replace existing values. In fact, if you want to completely replace the contents of cells, you can use the techniques from the previous section—whatever was in the cells prior to using that technique is simply replaced. It gets a little trickier when you want to replace only a portion of what is in the cell.

As an example, let's say that you want to go through a group of cells and replace any instances of "Widgets International" with "MegaWidgets Worldwide." All you need to do is take a look at the contents of the cell before making the change:

```
Dim ManyCells As Range
Dim c As Range
Dim sTemp As String
Dim sOld As String
Dim sNew As String

Set ManyCells = Range("A1:P250")
sOld = "Widgets International"
sNew = "Widgets Worldwide"

For Each c In ManyCells
    sTemp = c.Value
    If InStr(sTemp, sOld) Then
        sTemp = Replace(sTemp, sOld, sNew)
        c.Value = sTemp
    End If
Next c
```

The heart of this example is the For … Next loop, which examines each cell in the range. The Value property of each cell is placed in the sTemp variable, and then VBP's Replace function is used to make replacements of the old company name with the new company name. The altered value is then placed back into the Value property of the cell.

Getting Rid of Values

As you are editing your Excel workbooks, one of the most common actions to take is to clear or delete cells. *Clearing* cells means erasing everything within them, whereas *deleting* actually deletes the entire cell (or cells). In this section you discover how to clear cells, but deleting cells is best left to Chapter 11, where you discover how to affect your worksheet's structure.

VBA allows you to clear cells very, very quickly. Consider the following simple statement:

```
Selection.Clear
```

This simple statement clears everything from the cells that make up the current selection. You could also apply the same technique to a defined Range object, in this manner:

```
ManyCells.Clear
```

After execution, the cells are blank—their contents wiped out, their formats set back to default, and their comments stripped away.

If you'd prefer to only clear a portion of each cell you can replace the Clear method with one of the following methods:

- **Comments.** To clear any comments attached to the cells in the range (and only those comments), use the ClearComments method.

- **Contents.** To clear only the contents of the cells in the range, use the ClearContents method.

- **Formats.** To clear only the formatting from the range, use the ClearFormats method.

- **Hyperlinks.** To clear any hyperlinks in any of the cells, use the ClearHyperlinks method.

- **Notes.** Use the ClearNotes method to clear any notes associated with the cells.

- **Outline.** To clear any outlining applied to the cells, use the ClearOutline method.

As an example, let's say you wanted to just clear the formatting from whatever cells were selected when your macro was executed. You could use this single line:

```
Selection.ClearFormats
```

Affecting Formatting of a Range or Selection

You can use your macros to change the formatting used in a range or selection. In this way you can use your macro to affect not only what is in a range, but how the information in that range is presented in the worksheet.

When you work with the formatting of cells in a range or selection, there are two primary properties with which you will work:

- **Interior.** This property returns an object that represents the interior of a cell. (Many objects in Excel have interiors, and the Interior property can be used with them, as well. However, for formatting worksheets, you'll typically only work with the interior of individual cells.)

- **Font.** This property returns an object that represents the font of the characters that appear in the cell.

As an example of how these properties are used, let's say that you wanted to set the color of cell G6 to blue. (You'll discover more about colors shortly. Bear with me for the sake of example for right now.) You could use the following line:

```
Range("G6").Interior.Color = vbBlue
```

This sets the Color property of the Interior object for the range of cell G6 equal to blue.

The number of properties that determine how Excel displays information seems, at times, limitless. Chances are good that you won't need to use most of the formatting properties, but there are a few that will definitely come in handy. The following sections explain how to change some of the more common formatting characteristics of ranges and selections.

Making a Cell's Contents Bold or Italic

One of the more common formatting requirements is to change whether information is displayed using bold or italics. You do this by setting the Bold property of the Font object for a selection.

For instance, if you wanted to make the contents of cell A1 bold, you could use the following in your macro:

```
Cells(1, 1).Font.Bold = True
```

Likewise, if you wanted to make the currently selected cell bold, you could use the following code:

```
Selection.Font.Bold = True
```

If you wanted to explicitly turn off the bold attribute of a particular cell or range of cells, all you need to do is change True to False in the foregoing examples.

It is just as easy to format cell contents using italics, the only difference is that you use the Italic property of the Font object. All you need to do is replace the Bold property in the above examples with the Italic property, as shown here:

```
Cells(1, 1).Font.Italic = True
```

Working with Cell Colors

In versions of Excel up through Excel 2003, the program uses a color palette consisting of 56 colors. Starting with Excel 2007, this color palette was essentially thrown out of the window, as you'll discover shortly. First, however, let's see how you work with colors using VBA in older versions of Excel.

VBA provides the ColorIndex property, which can be applied to the Interior property of a single Cell object. As an example, the following macro displays the interior cell color used for each cell in a selection:

```
Sub ShowColors()
    Dim c As Range
    Dim sTemp As String

    sTemp = "Colors in the selection" & vbCrLf & vbCrLf

    For Each c In Selection
        sTemp = sTemp & c.Address & ": "
        sTemp = sTemp & c.Interior.ColorIndex & vbCrLf
    Next c
    MsgBox sTemp
End Sub
```

If you prefer to know the color used by whatever characters are in the cell instead of the actual color of the cell's interior, then simply replace the word "Interior" in the above with the word "Font". (Both the Interior property and the Font property, in turn, have their own ColorIndex property.)

If you run this macro, you quickly discover that ColorIndex is a number—it is an index value into the color palette used by Excel. Thus, a ColorIndex of 1 is the first color in the palette, 2 is the second, and so on.

Beginning with Excel 2007, the value of the ColorIndex property became essentially worthless. This is because starting with this version, Excel was no longer limited to the 56 colors in the color palette. Now the Color property (applicable to both the Interior and Font properties) is more important.

The Color property has been available in VBA all along, but in older versions of the program it was much more limited than it is in later versions, simply because later versions of Excel can handle more colors than older versions. In fact, the Color property can handle a value between 0 and 16,777,215— essentially 16 million colors!

Of course, nobody can remember that many color numbers, so the normal way most programmers set colors is to use the RGB function, in this manner:

```
Range("A3").Interior.Color = RGB(128, 0, 128)
```

How you use the RGB function is easy to remember: the order of the colors matches the letters in the function name. Thus, the first number represents the amount of red (0 through 255), the second is the amount of green (again, 0 through 255), and the third is the amount of blue (also 0 through 255).

If you prefer not to figure out the RGB values for whatever colors you desire, you can, instead, use the old-style VBA constants for some basic colors: vbBlack, vbWhite, vbRed, vbGreen, vbBlue, vbYellow, vbMagenta, and vbCyan. The ease of using these colors is why you see so many instances of them within worksheets formatted using macros:

```
Range("A3").Interior.Color = vbRed
```

Checking for Cell Color

Excel has two different types of formatting that can be applied to cell. The first is explicit formatting. This type of formatting is applied by using the tools on the ribbon tabs or by using the Cells option from the Format menu. The second type of formatting is conditional formatting. This type of formatting is applied based on a set of rules that you define.

It is important to understand that these two types of formatting are separate and distinct from each other. For instance, if you explicitly format a cell as bold red, that is the way it appears. If you later apply a conditional format to it, and that format causes the cell to appear in green, that is exactly what is happening—the cell is appearing in green, but it is still formatted as red.

What does this have to do with VBA? If you test the formatting of a cell in VBA, then the formatting you are testing is the explicit formatting. In the above scenario, this means that the test will always indicate that the cell is bold red and never report that it is green, regardless of what the conditional formatting is doing to the cell. This is because conditional formatting affects the cell's display, not its underlying (explicit) formatting.

The other upshot of all this is that if you want to find out what conditional formatting is being displayed, you may need to recreate all your conditional tests within VBA. This can get rather complex rather quickly. For more information on this topic, there is a great page you can refer to. Check out one of Chip Pearson's pages, here:

http://www.cpearson.com/excel/CFColors.htm

Applying Custom Formatting

Those who have been around Excel for any length of time understand that it includes a feature know as custom formatting. This simply means that you can create your own formatting for cells in your worksheet. How you use custom formatting is a topic beyond the scope of this book, but one thing you do need to know is that you can apply custom formatting to a cell (or range of cells) using VBA.

If you want to do any work with formatting, you'll want to become familiar with the NumberFormat property. You can read this property to discover what formatting is applied to a cell, as shown here:

```
Dim r As Range
Dim sTemp As String

Set r = Range("B6")
sTemp = r.NumberFormat
MsgBox sTemp
```

What is displayed in the resulting message box is the underlying custom format for cell B6. This is the same format you'd see if you display the Format Cells dialog box, display the Number tab, and then click Custom.

You can also read the NumberFormat for a range of cells, but what you get back may not be what you expect. If all the cells use the same formatting, then you get back the formatting, the same as if you had examined the NumberFormat property for a single cell in the range. If, however, there are multiple formats used within the range, then the function returns a null value. Because of this, it is a a good idea to check to see if the property returns a null value:

```
Dim r As Range
Dim sTemp As String

Set r = Range("B5:B6")
sTemp = r.NumberFormat
If IsNull(sTemp) Then
    sTemp = "Not defined or mixed formatting"
End If
MsgBox sTemp
```

In this example if a null value is returned (as tested by the IsNull function), then a message is displayed instead of the format.

How you set formats using the NumberFormat property is rather easy. All you need to do is put together a string that represents the formatting template you want applied. Information on how to use custom formatting codes is available in any good Excel reference or on the ExcelTips website. A quick example should suffice for now, however:

```
Selection.NumberFormat = "d mmm"
```

This example sets the formatting for the selected cells to be the day of the month, followed by a space, followed by the three-character abbreviation for the month.

The Text Method

So far in this chapter, whenever you've examined cell contents, you've used the Value method. This allows you to get to what is actually stored in a cell, as in the following:

```
Dim c As Range
Dim sTemp As String

For Each c In Selection
    If (c.Value) > 1000 Then
        sTemp = "Value is too high in "
        sTemp = sTemp & c.Address
        MsgBox sTemp
    End If
Next c
```

Excel also provides the Text method to derive what is in a cell. The difference between the Value method and the Text method is that the Text method returns the formatted value of the cell. Thus, if a cell contains the value of 1234.56, then the Text method may return "$1,234.56" if the cell is formatted to include thousands separators and a currency indicator.

To see how this works, try this little macro:

```
Sub LookInCell()
    Dim vContent As Variant
    Dim sContent As String
    Dim sTemp As String

    vContent = Selection.Value
    sContent = Selection.Text
    sTemp = "Cell value: " & vContent & vbCrLf
    sTemp = sTemp & "Cell text:   " & sContent
    MsgBox sTemp
End Sub
```

When you select a cell and run the macro, a message box is displayed that shows both the contents of the cell as returned by both the Value method and the Text method. (Figure 10-1 shows an example of the message box.)

You should choose to use the Text method when it is important for your macro to be aware of how the value within a cell is formatted. There is another big difference between Value and Text properties, however: The Value property can be both read and written to, but the Text property can only be

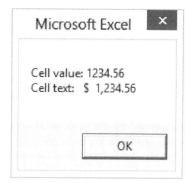

Figure 10-1. The Value and Text methods can return a cell's content differently.

read. Thus, if you want to store a value in a cell, you must use the Value property; Text won't work for that purpose.

Discovering Information about a Range or Selection

Excel allows a variety of information to be stored in individual cells. The basics of what you can store are three-fold: formulas, numbers, and text. (Some people might protest and say that you can store dates and times, as well, but those are still simply numbers. They are displayed as dates and times based on the formatting applied to the cell.)

When processing information in a worksheet, it is helpful to know what is in the cell. The following sections provide some helpful information in this regard.

Getting Information Using VBA Functions

VBA provides a variety of functions that can be used to determine the characteristics of what is contained within a range or selection. These functions are normally used to test what is in VBA variables, but they can also be used to examine the contents of cells in a range. The most useful of these functions include these:

- **IsDate.** Determines whether an expression can be converted to a date or time.

- **IsEmpty.** Determines if an expression has ever been initialized or not.

- **IsNull.** Determines if an expression contains no valid data.

- **IsNumeric.** Determines if an expression can be evaluated as a number.

These functions each return either True or False, and can thus be used very easily in testing cell contents. As an example, let's say that you want to check whatever is in cell B9. If it is 0, then you want to color the cell red. If it is anything else—including empty—then you want there to be no color in the cell.

```
Sub CheckForZero()
    Dim r As Range
    Set r = Range("B9")

    r.Interior.Color = xlNone
    If (Not IsEmpty(r)) _
      And IsNumeric(r) _
      And (r.Value = 0) Then
        r.Interior.Color = vbRed
    End If
End Sub
```

This macro actually checks three conditions: that B9 is not empty (uses the IsEmpty function), that it contains a numeric value (uses the IsNumeric function), and that the value is 0. If all three of these conditions are met, then the interior color of B9 is set to red.

Getting Information Using VBA Methods

Excel also provides, through VBA, a number of different methods that can be used to determine information about what is stored in a cell. These are the most useful of these methods:

- **IsNumber.** This method belongs to the Application object and is primarily used to determine whether a varibable contains a number or not. It can, however, be just as easily used to determine if a particular cell contains a number. The IsNumber method returns True or False, depending on whether the variable or cell contains a number.

- **IsText.** This method also belongs to the Application object. As its name implies, it returns True or False based on whether the cell or variable being evaluated contains a text string or not.

- **HasFormula.** This method belongs to a Range object, which means it applies specifically to cell contents. It returns True or False, depending on whether the cell contains a formula. If the Range object contains more than a single cell and some of the cells contain formulas and others don't, then the HasFormula method returns a Null value.

- **Address.** This method also belongs to a Range object and returns the absolute address of the cell or the address of the range of cells. Thus, the address returns something like $A$7 or $D$3:$F$12.

How Many Cells are There?

One of the most often-used informational properties is the Count property. This property can be applied to a large number of objects in Excel VBA, and is typically associated with collections of objects. For instance, the following assigns to the ct variable the number of worksheets in the workbook:

```
ct = Worksheets.Count
```

The place that most people don't think of using the Count property, however, is with a Range object. Just as described above, Count returns the number of cells in the Range object. This can be very helpful when your code needs to perform different tasks based on the number of cells in the range.

```
Dim sTemp As String

sTemp = "There "
If Selection.Count > 1 then
    sTemp = sTemp & "are " & Selection.Count & " cells"
Else
    sTemp = sTemp & "is one cell"
End If
sTemp = sTemp & " in the selected range."
MsgBox sTemp
```

Working with Named Ranges

One of the powerful features of Excel is the ability to, within a workbook, create named ranges. You can select a cell or range of cells and then give that range of name that can then be used within formulas and functions to refer to that range.

VBA makes it very easy to reference those named ranges within your macros. In fact, there are several ways you can access the range, using either the Range object or the Names collection.

To access the named range using the Range object, all you need to do is provide the name of the range as a parameter to the object. This name is the same one that you defined within Excel. For instance, the following line could be used to change the interior color of the entire range:

```
Worksheets("Sheet1").Range("Account").Interior.Color = vbYellow
```

Note that the Range object is used relative to a particular worksheet, in this case Sheet1. As a parameter to the Range object you provide the name of the range (Account) as defined within the worksheet. You could also define a range object within VBA and then assign it to be equal to the named range, in this manner:

```
Dim rng As Range

Set rng = Worksheets("Sheet1").Range("Account")
```

Once the rng variable is set, you can work with that range the same as any other range you might create in VBA.

The other method of using the named range is to use the Names collection. The following line will again set the interior color of the range to yellow:

```
Workbooks("Book1.xlsx").Names("Account").RefersToRange.Interior.Color =
vbYellow
```

Note that the Names collection is relative to the entire workbook, so it is not necessary to know which worksheet the named range is associated with when you use this method of access. It is the RefersToRange property that actually does the heavy lifting in this approach; it returns the actual range object that is referred to by the named range.

You can also define a range object in VBA and assign it to be the same as the named range:

```
Dim rng As Range

Set rng = Workbooks("Book1.xlsx").Names("Account").RefersToRange
```

You should know that the Names collection method of accessing a named range will only be viable if you don't have the same named range defined on different worksheets in the workbook. If you do, then you will need to use the Range object method, which requires the use of a specific worksheet name in the reference.

Adding a Named Range

As with other objects in VBA, you can add a named range within your macro by simply using the Add method with the Names collection. In order to create the named range, though, you need to provide—at a minimum—a name for the range and the cells that it references.

```
Names.Add Name:="MyRange", RefersTo:="=Sheet1!$M$3:$M$7"
```

When done, the MyRange named range is defined and can be accessed from within the workbook.

You should be careful when adding named ranges that you don't use a given name more than once. For instance, the following should theoretically work:

```
Names.Add Name:="MyRange", RefersTo:="=Sheet1!$M$3:$M$7"
Names.Add Name:="MyRange", RefersTo:="=Sheet1!$J$12:$J$15"
```

What you may think will happen is that the second invocation of the Add method will overwrite the previous invocation, so that you end up with only one MyRange named range. In fact, that is what you will see when you later examine the contents of the Names collection, and in Excel you'll see the last instance of Add reflected in the Name Manger.

However, in practice I've discovered that you may get some wonky results after the duplicate Add method is executed. I found that the names in the Name Manager would proliferate, on their own, without any rhyme or reason. (This didn't occur before the second Add invocation.)

Instead, it is better to check to see if a particular name is in use before using the Add method. If it is in use, then simply modify the name in some way so that whatever you are adding is unique. You could always, of course delete the existing named range before adding it back again with the same name.

Deleting a Named Range

In order to get rid of a named range in VBA, you use the Delete method. However, this method isn't used with the Names collection, but with individual items within the Names collection. (This makes logical sense—you add items to the collection, but you delete individual items from the collection.)

The simplest way to use the Delete method is in this manner:

```
Names("MyRange").Delete
```

If you want to delete all of the named ranges in a workbook, then you can use a simple For Each loop:

```
Dim n As Name

For Each n In Names
    n.Delete
Next n
```

Remember that deleting a named range doesn't get rid of the data that was in the range, it only gets rid of the name that references the range.

Displaying Information about Named Ranges

Each Name object within the Names collection has a variety of properties that can be associated with that object. In fact, at last check there were 20 different properties that run the gamut from the object's index number (in the Names collection) to information about any shortcut key associated with the object.

Normally, most of these properties will be of little or marginal value to you, unless you are doing some pretty heavy-duty work with named ranges. There are a few properties that may come in handy, however, including the following:

- **Index:** The ID of the named range within the Names collection.
- **Name:** The name assigned to the named range.
- **RefersTo:** The ranged referred to by the named range.
- **Value:** The value associated with the named range. (Typically, RefersTo and Value are synonymous.)

You can easily create a macro that will step through each Name object in the Names collection and display information about that particular object.

```
Dim n As Name
Dim sTemp As String

sTemp = "There are " & Names.Count & " named ranges in the workbook."
MsgBox sTemp

For Each n In Names
    sTemp = n.Name & "(" & n.Index & "): "
    sTemp = sTemp & n.RefersTo & vbCrLf
    sTemp = sTemp & n.Value
    MsgBox sTemp
Next n
```

Using Ranges to Remember User Locations

When creating macros that require changing what is selected in the workbook, it is good programming form to make sure you save whatever the user had selected before your macro was executed. This is particularly important if your macro could change to a different worksheet, leaving the user confused as to what he or she is seeing when the macro is completed.

For the best chance of getting someone back to where they where before your macro started, there are three elements you need to be concerned with: workbook, worksheet, and cell. Actually, this last element (cell) may be a bit simplistic, as the user will always have a cell selected, but may additionally have a range selected.

Using the information presented in this chapter (and some not actually discussed in detail until the next chapter), here's how you get all four items:

```
Dim rngOrigSelection As Range
Dim rngOrigCell As Range
Dim sOrigWS As String
Dim sOrigWB As String

Set rngOrigSelection = Selection
Set rngOrigCell = ActiveCell
sOrigWS = ActiveSheet.Name
sOrigWB = ActiveWorkbook.Name
```

When you want to later return the user to where they were, you can use this type of code:

```
Workbooks(sOrigWB).Activate
Sheets(sOrigWS).Select
rngOrigSelection.Select
rngOrigCell.Activate
```

Of course, Excel always has multiple ways that you can accomplish any given task. In this case, you could shorten your code by only remembering the active cell and selected range:

```
Dim rngOrigSelection As Range
Dim rngOrigCell As Range

Set rngOrigSelection = Selection
Set rngOrigCell = ActiveCell
```

When you want to restore the user to the location, you rely upon the Parent object available in VBA:

```
rngOrigSelection.Parent.Parent.Activate
rngOrigSelection.Parent.Select
rngOrigSelection.Select
rngOrigCell.Activate
```

The Parent object of the selection range you saved is the worksheet in which that range is located, and the Parent of that Parent object is the workbook in which the worksheet is located.

Another approach is to simply create, within your macro, a named range that refers to whatever the user had selected:

```
ActiveWorkbook.Names.Add Name:="MyOrigPlace", RefersTo:=Selection
```

After you do your processing, when you are ready to return to what the user had selected, you use this code:

```
Application.Goto Reference:="MyOrigPlace"
ActiveWorkbook.Names("MyOrigPlace").Delete
```

The first line returns to the selection (stored in the MyOrigPlace named range) and the second line then deletes the named range. The only drawback to this approach is that the active cell is not retained; the code assumes that you want the upper-left cell in the range to be the active cell when it is done. You should also be aware that if your processing deletes the cells that make up the named range, then the code may not work properly—Excel can't go to a place that no longer exists.

Of course, you may not have to remember any location at all, if you code your macro correctly. While VBA allows you to "move around" and select different areas of your worksheets and workbook, in most cases this isn't necessary. You could, for instance, simply work with different ranges and then do your work on those ranges, without ever changing the current selection or active cell. Indeed, VBA allows you to change, reformat, sort, delete, and do almost anything you can imagine to cells without actually needing to select them.

Understanding Excel's Special Cells

You already know that a Range object is used to refer to a collection of cells in a worksheet. Most of the time the Range objects you create will refer to contiguous ranges of cells, as in B7:G25 or F3:F19. Excel does provide a method that allows you to create a Range object that refers to cells within a contiguous range that all share something in common.

As an example, let's say that you wanted to select all the cells within A1:E100 that are empty. You could use the following:

```
Range("A1:E100").SpecialCells(xlCellTypeBlanks).Select
```

The SpecialCells method specifies, in this instance, that you want all the cells that don't have anyting in them. All in all, Excel allows you to grab cells that fall into six different categories:

- **xlCellTypeBlanks.** Returns only those cells which contain nothing.
- **xlCellTypeComments.** Returns only the cells that have comments associated with them.
- **xlCellTypeConstants.** Returns only the cells that contain constants, such as 2, 3, 18, or anoter explicit value.

- **xlCellTypeFormulas.** Returns only cells that contain formulas in them.

- **xlCellTypeLastCell.** Returns the last (bottom right) cell in the range.

- **xlCellTypeVisible.** Returns only those cells which are currently visible.

In addition, if you want either constants or formulas, Excel allows you to specify a second parameter that indicates what type of constants or formulas you are interested in. Here are the secondary parameters:

- **xlNumbers.** Those cells that contain only numeric values.

- **xlTextValues.** Those cells containing text.

- **xlLogical.** Those cells that contain logical values, such as True or False.

- **xlErrors.** Those cells that contain error values.

These secondary parameters can be combined together, as well. For instance, if you wanted a Range object that contained all the cells in the current selection that contain only text and numeric constants, you could use the following:

```
Dim rng As Range

Set rng = Selection.SpecialCells(xlCellTypeConstants, xlNumbers +
xlTextValues)
```

11

Working with Worksheets

The data you place in an Excel workbook is stored in any number of worksheets. This means that understanding how to work with worksheets is fundamental to doing just about anything in Excel. This chapter discusses how you can utilize the power of VBA to do just about anything you can think of with worksheets. Here you learn quite a bit about working with worksheets:

- What the Worksheet object is and how you use it.
- How to create, access, and delete Worksheet objects
- Ways you can copy, move, and even hide Worksheet objects
- How to merge cells
- How you can both insert and delete cells, rows, and columns
- Editing worksheet contents by cutting, copying, and pasting
- How to adjust row height and column width

The Worksheet Object

Those who have used Excel for any length of time—even in passing—know that individual workbooks are composed of worksheets. A workbook can contain any number of worksheets, and in VBA those worksheets are each represented by a Worksheet object. This structure becomes very noticeable when you examine a workbook and its worksheets in the Project Explorer, shown in Figure 11-1.

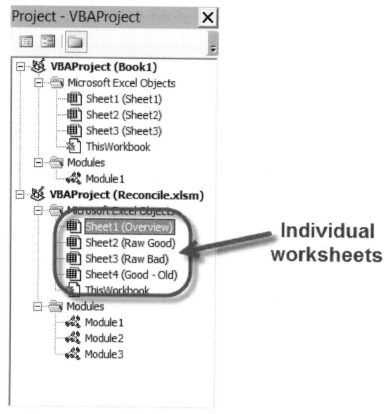

Figure 11-1. *Worksheet objects represent individual worksheets in a workbook.*

Worksheet objects are part of the Worksheets collection. Excel allows you to have open, at any given time, any number of worksheets, so the Worksheets collection can contain any number of Worksheet objects.

There are three object collections that are easy to get confused. (Well, two of them are easy to get confused.) These are the Worksheets collection, the Sheets collection, and the Charts collection. The easiest way to stop from getting confused is to remember that the Worksheets and Charts collections are actually subsets of the Sheets collection:

- The Sheets collection is all of the sheets in a workbook, of any type.

- The Worksheets collection is all of the standard worksheets in the workbook.

- The Charts collection is all of the sheet-sized charts in the workbook.

Many times you'll examine people's code and see them use the Sheets collection and the Worksheets collection almost interchangeably. For the simplest workbooks, this is fine, but it can lead to problems in more complicated workbooks. When you want to refer specficially to worksheets (as we do in this chapter) it is best to be explicit and always reference the Worksheets collection.

Creating New Worksheets

The way that you you add new worksheets to a workbook is straightforward in VBA—you simply use the Add method with the Worksheets collection. The simplest way to create a worksheet is as follows:

```
Worksheets.Add
```

Used in this way, the Add method creates a new Worksheet object and adds it to the Worksheets collection. The worksheet represented by the object is automatically added just before whichever worksheet has focus in the workbook. If you want to make sure that the new worksheet is added elsewhere in the range of existing worksheets, all you need to do is specify a "before" or "after" setting.

Before getting to those particular settings, it is good to keep in mind that Excel actually allows you to use any of four optional parameters with the Add method. These parameters, in order, as as follows:

- **Before.** Used to specify the worksheet before which you want the new worksheet added. Cannot be used if you specify the After parameter.

- **After.** Used to specify the worksheet after which you want the new worksheet added. Cannot be used if you specify the Before parameter.

- **Count.** The number of worksheets to add. (Defaults to one worksheet.)

- **Type.** Specifies the type of sheet you want added. Can be xlWorksheet (the default), xlChart, xlExcel4MacroSheet, or xlExcel4IntlMacroSheet. The first two are the most commonly used and the last two are slowly being phased out by Microsoft.

Since these parameters are in order, if you wanted to add a worksheet after an existing worksheet named February, you could do the following:

```
Worksheets.Add(,"February")
```

Note the use of the leading comma within the parentheses. This is because, again, of the order of the parameters; the first parameter (Before) doesn't matter, but we want Excel to know that "February" is the After parameter. Another way you can accomplish this task is in this manner:

```
Worksheets.Add After:="February"
```

The combination of a colon and an equal sign let's Excel know that you are assigning a value to a specific parameter to be used by the Add method.

As an example of how you can add worksheets in a macro, take a look at the AddMonths macro:

```
Sub AddMonths()
    Dim J As Integer
    Dim K As Integer
    Dim sTemp As String
    Dim sMo(12) As String

    sMo(1) = "January"
    sMo(2) = "February"
    sMo(3) = "March"
    sMo(4) = "April"
    sMo(5) = "May"
    sMo(6) = "June"
    sMo(7) = "July"
    sMo(8) = "August"
    sMo(9) = "September"
    sMo(10) = "October"
    sMo(11) = "November"
    sMo(12) = "December"

    'Make sure there are no worksheets already having month names
    For J = 1 To Worksheets.Count
        sTemp = Worksheets(J).Name
        For K = 1 To 12
            If sTemp = sMo(K) Then
                sMo(K) = ""
            End If
```

```
        Next K
    Next J

    For J = 1 To 12
        'Only add worksheet if it doesn't already exist
        If sMo(J) > "" Then
            Worksheets.Add After:=Worksheets(Worksheets.Count)
            ActiveSheet.Name = sMo(J)
        End If
    Next J

    Worksheets(1).Activate
End Sub
```

Note that the heart of the macro, where a worksheet is actually added, specifies the After parameter as equal to whatever the last worksheet in the workbook is. (The Count property in this case returns the number of worksheets—a number—which is used as an index to the Worksheets collection. This technique always refers to the last worksheet in the workbook.)

Accessing Worksheets

It is only once in a great while that a workbook will have a single worksheet. For this reason, you need to have a way to specify which worksheet you actually want to work with. There are three common ways to do this: assign variables, use indexes, and use the ActiveSheet object.

One common way to keep track of the worksheet you are using is to use variables. Consider the following example:

```
Dim wsTarget As Worksheet

Set wsTarget = Worksheets.Add
```

This code sets the wsTarget variable so that it references a newly added worksheet. From this point on, you can use the wsTarget variable to reference this worksheet, separate from all other worksheets in the Worksheets collection.

Speaking of the Worksheets collection, you can also use an index into the collection to refer to individual worksheets:

```
Dim wsTarget As Worksheet

Set wsTarget = Worksheets(4)
```

This code sets the wsTarget variable so that it references the fourth Worksheet object in the Worksheets collection. You can't always count on the Worksheet objects to be in any particular order in the Worksheets collection, which presents a problem with this indexing method. A more precise approach is to use the name of a worksheet as its index:

```
Dim wsTarget As Worksheet

Set wsTarget = Worksheets("Expenditures")
```

The final way that most people refer to individual worksheets is by using the ActiveSheet object. As its name implies, this object is always equal to whatever the currently active worksheet is.

A worksheet is considered to be active when it has focus. When you are working in a worksheet, if you can enter information into cells in a the worksheet, then it is active. You generally switch between worksheets (and thereby change which one is active) by clicking on the worksheet tabs at the bottom of the Excel program window.

In your macros you can activate a worksheet by using the Activate method, in this manner:

```
Dim wsTarget As Worksheet

Set wsTarget = Worksheets("Expenditures")
wsTarget.Activate
```

Copying Worksheets

When organizing data in workbooks, it is not uncommon to copy worksheets from one workbook to another. When creating a macro you can use the Copy method with an individual Worksheet object or with a group of worksheets. For instance, the following macro code will copy the currently selected worksheet to a new workbook:

```
ActiveSheet.Copy
```

That's it; a single line is all that is necessary to copy the worksheet to a new, unnamed workbook. After executing the line, the new workbook is selected and you can save it using code similar to the following. The first line in the code saves the workbook, and the second closes it.

```
ActiveWorkbook.SaveAs("NewFile.xlsm")
ActiveWindow.Close
```

If you want to copy a specific sheet to another workbook, you do it by specifying the name of the sheet you want to copy, instead of using the ActiveSheet object:

```
Worksheets("Sheet1").Copy
```

This example copies the worksheet named Sheet1, from the Worksheets collection, to a new workbook. You can then save the new workbook, as already discussed.

The Copy method, when used with worksheets, is not limited to copying a single sheet at a time. If you have a group of sheets selected, you can still use a single command line to copy all of them to a new workbook. That is what is done in the following macro:

```
Sub CopyWorkbook()
    Dim sCopyName As String

    sCopyName = "My New Workbook.xlsx"

    ActiveWindow.SelectedSheets.Copy
    ActiveWorkbook.SaveAs(sCopyName)
End Sub
```

Note the use of the Copy command. The macro will work whether you have one worksheet selected or fifty; it doesn't matter. If you wanted to, instead, copy all of the worksheets from one workbook to another, all you need to do is make a single change in the macro, to the line where the Copy method is invoked:

```
Worksheets.Copy
```

This copies the entire Worksheets collection, which consists of all the worksheets in the workbook.

It should be noted that the Copy method isn't just for copying worksheets to a new workbook; it can also be used to copy worksheets within the same workbook. The only thing you need to do is specify where in the current workbook you want to make the copy:

```
ActiveSheet.Copy After:=Worksheets("Sheet7")
```

This code line copies the active worksheet into the same workbook so that it appears after the worksheet named Sheet7. If it is more appropriate for your needs, you could instead specify the worksheet before which the copy should be placed:

```
ActiveSheet.Copy Before:=Sheets("Sheet7")
```

This results in the worksheet being placed before Sheet7 instead of after it. Here's another example that places the worksheet copy as the last sheet in the workbook:

```
Worksheets("Master").Copy After:=Worksheets(Worksheets.Count)
```

Moving Worksheets

Closely related to the Copy method (in the preceding section) is the Move method. This method allows you to adjust the order of worksheets within a workbook. Just like the Copy method, the Move method allows you to specify a Before or After parameter that indicates where you want the worksheet located. Unlike the Copy method, however, the Move method requires one of these parameters.

As an example of how to use the Move method, consider the following macro which quickly sorts all the worksheets in a workbook:

```
Sub SortSheets()
    Dim J As Integer
    Dim K As Integer

    For J = 1 To Sheets.Count - 1
        For K = J + 1 To Sheets.Count
            If UCase(Worksheets(J).Name) > UCase(Worksheets(K).Name) Then
                Worksheets(K).Move Before:=Worksheets(J)
            End If
        Next K
    Next J
End Sub
```

Note how the Move property is used with the Before parameter to specify the final location of where you want the worksheet moved.

Deleting Worksheets

Deleting a worksheet is just as easy as adding one. For example, you can use the following code to delete the active worksheet:

```
ActiveSheet.Delete
```

If you issue the command in your macro, you will find that Excel pauses the macro and asks you if you are sure you want to delete the worksheet. When you click on Yes, the worksheet is deleted and the macro resumes.

The whole idea behind macros, of course, is to automate many of the tasks you do on a regular basis. Stopping and asking for confirmation may be the safe way to go, but it doesn't do much to help the cause of automation. If you want the worksheet to be deleted without a pause, the solution is to turn off the alerting capabilities of Excel for a short time. Consider the following macro code:

```
Application.DisplayAlerts = False
Worksheets("Summary").Delete
Application.DisplayAlerts = True
```

This code turns off the alerts, deletes the worksheet named Summary, and then turns the alerts back on. While they are turned off, Excel will not display the confirmation dialog box, but will act as if it had been displayed and the default option (Yes) selected.

It is important to remember the last line of code shown here. If you do not set the DisplayAlerts property back to True, then Excel will not show any more alert messages, even after the macro has ended. This could cause problems, as you might imagine. It is best to only set it to False for the short time you need the alerts turned off.

Even with DisplayAlerts set to False, you will still see error messages, if one is generated. For instance, if you execute the above code and there is no worksheet named Summary or if there is one and it is the only worksheet in the workbook, you will still see an error message.

Hiding Worksheets

You may already know that Excel allows you to hide worksheets so that they don't have a tab at the bottom of the Excel program window. Hiding a worksheet (or multiple worksheets) is often done to protect the information that is stored on it (or them). After all, it is much harder to accidently change or delete information if you can't easily display it.

In VBA, whether a worksheet is hidden or not is controlled by the Visible property. For instance, this code sets the workbook named *Important Stuff* so that it is hidden:

```
Worksheets("Important Stuff").Visible = False
```

A worksheet that has its Visible property set to False can be easily displayed, again, by the user just by unhiding the worksheet. (The steps to unhide worksheets aren't difficult, but they do vary from version to version of Excel.) Interestingly, Excel provides a way to make a worksheet "super hidden," so to speak:

```
Worksheets("Super Important Stuff").Visible = xlVeryHidden
```

You can also use the constant xlSheetVeryHidden, which is a synonym for xlVeryHidden. The worksheet still shows up when you are stepping through the Worksheets collection, but it doesn't show up as a worksheet that the user can unhide—it must be done in a maco by setting the Visible property back to True.

That being said, if you want to process information on a hidden (or very hidden) worksheet, you'll want to make sure that you reference the worksheet using a variable that you've set properly. You'll also want to keep in mind that you should work with Range objects on the worksheet, not with Selection objects. (See Chapter 10 for information about working with Range and Selection objects.)

Adjusting Worksheet Structure

We all know the general structure of a worksheet: It includes a series of rows and columns, the intersection of which constitutes a cell. While you can't change this basic structure, you can use VBA to perform tasks that are part and parcel of adjusting the structure of your data within those rows and columns.

The following sections detail the majority of the structural tasks you can take care of in VBA. You discover how to merge and unmerge cells; insert and delete rows, columns, and cells; and how to adjust row height and column width.

Merging Cells

When you define a Range object that contains more than one contiguous cell or have a Selection object that refers to more than one contiguous cell, then you can merge those cells so they are treated as a single cell. The way you do it is simple; just use the Merge method:

```
Dim r As Range

Set r = Range("D7:G10")
r.Merge
```

This code results in the cells originally at D7:G10 being merged. The results are shown in Figure 11-2.

When you merge cells and there is information in the "before" cells, then Excel displays a message that you will lose the data in the cells, keeping only the data in the cell at the upper-left corner of the range being merged.

How you interact with merged cells is rather strange in Excel. Consider the following code:

```
Dim r As Range
Dim s As Range

Set r = Range("B3:F3")
r.Merge

Set s = Range("E3")
MsgBox s.Address

s.Select
MsgBox Selection.Address
```

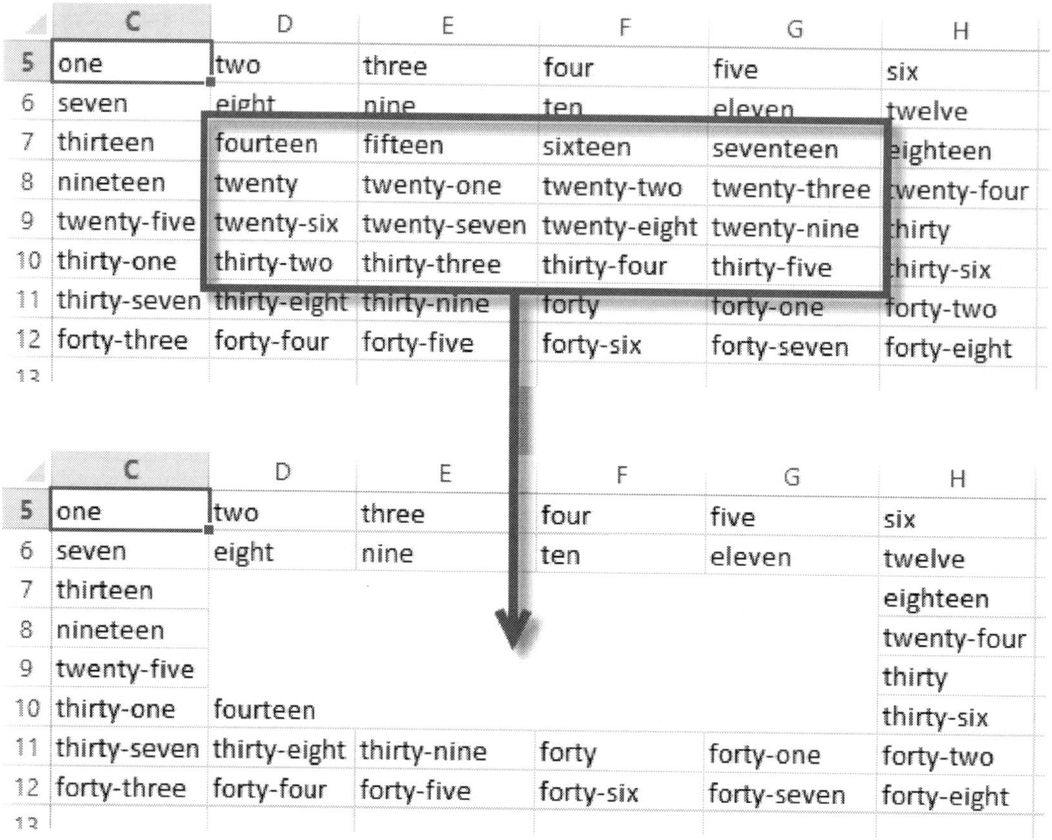

	C	D	E	F	G	H
5	one	two	three	four	five	six
6	seven	eight	nine	ten	eleven	twelve
7	thirteen	fourteen	fifteen	sixteen	seventeen	eighteen
8	nineteen	twenty	twenty-one	twenty-two	twenty-three	twenty-four
9	twenty-five	twenty-six	twenty-seven	twenty-eight	twenty-nine	thirty
10	thirty-one	thirty-two	thirty-three	thirty-four	thirty-five	thirty-six
11	thirty-seven	thirty-eight	thirty-nine	forty	forty-one	forty-two
12	forty-three	forty-four	forty-five	forty-six	forty-seven	forty-eight
13						

	C	D	E	F	G	H
5	one	two	three	four	five	six
6	seven	eight	nine	ten	eleven	twelve
7	thirteen					eighteen
8	nineteen					twenty-four
9	twenty-five					thirty
10	thirty-one	fourteen				thirty-six
11	thirty-seven	thirty-eight	thirty-nine	forty	forty-one	forty-two
12	forty-three	forty-four	forty-five	forty-six	forty-seven	forty-eight
13						

Figure 11-2. *Cells before and after a cell merge.*

If you run this code, you'll notice something odd: The first message box displays an address of $E$3 and the second message box displays an address of $B$3:$F$3. In other words, a Range object can refer to a cell within a merged group of cells, but a Selection cannot; it can only refer to the entire merged group.

This might lead you to believe, however, that you can assign values to individual cells within a merged group of cells, simply by assigning something to the Value property:

```
Dim r As Range
Dim s As Range
```

```
Set r = Range("B3:F3")
r.Merge

Set s = Range("E3")
s.Value = 27
```

This code won't work. It doesn't generate an error, but it also doesn't set the value of cell E3 to 27. You can only assign a value to the merged cells if you assign it to the cell in the upper-left corner of the merged group, as in this manner:

```
Dim r As Range
Dim s As Range

Set r = Range("B3:F3")
r.Merge

Set s = Range("B3")
s.Value = 27
```

When you want to unmerge a group of cells, the easiest way to do so is to simply select the merged cells (you can use the Select method to do this) and then use the UnMerge method:

```
Range("E3").Select    'Select any cell in the group of merged cells

Selection.UnMerge
```

Inserting Cells, Rows, and Columns

At the heart of editing the structure of any worksheet is the ability to insert and delete cells, rows, and columns. This section focuses on inserting, while the following section focuses on deleting.

To insert cells, you use the Insert method with either a Range or Selection object. Here's an example that inserts the cells in a range (ManyCells) and moves the displaced cells right to make room for the insertion:

```
ManyCells.Insert xlShiftToRight
```

When you insert cells into a workbook, Excel moves the cells defined by the range or selection (ManyCells in the above example) in order to make room for the blank cells being inserted. There are two directions that the displaced cells can be moved: to the right or downward. Interestingly enough, Excel provides four enumerations you can use for the two directions. To shift cells to the right you can use xlShiftToRight (as shown above) as well as xlToRight. To shift cells downward, you can use either xlShiftDown or xlDown.

If you want to insert an entire row, then you use the appropriately named EntireRow property just before the Insert method. For instance, if you wanted to insert four rows right after row 7, you could use the following:

```
Range(A7:A10).EntireRow.Insert
```

Inserting columns is just as easy, the only difference being that you use the EntireColumn property. Notice that you don't need to provide an indicator for direction when you are inserting either rows or columns. Excel always moves rows down and moves columns to the right.

Deleting Cells, Rows, and Columns

In Chapter 10 you discovered the difference between clearing and deleting cells. When you delete cells, you effectively remove those cells from the workbook. It is a rather drastic change to the structure of your worksheet. When you delete cells, they are removed entirely and the resulting cells in the worksheet are either moved left or moved up, depending on how you put together the command to get rid of the cells.

To delete cells, you use the Delete method with either a Range or Selection object. Here's an example that deletes all the cells in a range and moves the remaining cells left to fill the void:

```
ManyCells.Delete xlShiftToLeft
```

Interestingly enough, there are four different enumerations you can use with the Delete method. To shift cells to the left you can use xlShiftToLeft (as shown above) as well as xlToLeft. To shift cells up, you can use either xlShiftUp or xlUp.

When you want to delete an entire row or an entire column, all you need to do is include the EntireRow or EntireColumn property just before the Delete method. For instance, the following will delete rows 5 and 6 from the worksheet:

```
Range("A5:A6").EntireRow.Delete
```

There is no need to specify which way the remaining cells should shift, since deleting rows will always result in moving the remaining rows up. You can similarly delete entire columns by using the EntireColumn property:

```
Range("F1:J1").EntireColumn.Delete
```

This example deletes columns F:J from the worksheet.

Cutting, Copying, and Pasting

The real workhorses of moving information in Excel are the cut, copy, and paste functions. It is no surprise that these functions are placed prominently at the left side of the Home tab of the ribbon.

In VBA Excel provides both a Cut and Copy method that work quite nicely with either a range or selection. It does not, however, provide an immediately obvious method that pastes information. Instead, if you want to paste whatever you are copying or cutting, you simply make the destination part of the actual Cut or Copy methods.

For example, the following code copies the range F3:H7 to cell F53:

```
Range("F3:H7").Copy Range("F53")
```

The range being copied in this instance consists of five rows and three columns, for a total of 15 cells. When pasted at cell F53, the range still extends for five rows and three columns; cell F53 is assumed to be the upper-left corner of the target for the range.

Cutting information from one place to another is just as easy. All you need to do is substitute the Cut method for the Copy method:

```
Range("F3:H7").Cut Range("F53")
```

The Cut method requires the inclusion of a target, but the Copy method does not. If you use the Copy method without a target, then the specified range or selection is copied to the Clipboard.

With information in the Clipboard, you can then use a couple of ways to place that information somewhere else. The three major methods are the Paste method, the Insert method, and the PasteSpecial method.

First, a look at the Paste method. Interestingly, this method is not used with a Range object or a Selection object. Instead, it is used with the Worksheet object. In some ways this makes sense—you copy from a range and you paste into a worksheet. Here's an example:

```
Range("F3:H7").Copy
Range("F53").Select
ActiveWorksheet.Paste
```

Note that if you use this approach to pasting, you need to explicitly select a range before using the Paste method. Thus, it is shorter and more concise if you include the target with the Copy method, as describe earlier in this section, if the target is on the same worksheet as the source. If you are pasting to a location on a different worksheet, however, it is probably better to use the technique that uses the Paste method.

The second technique is to use the Insert method (described earlier in this chapter) to paste the information elsewhere in the worksheet. For instance, the following code copies the current row and then pastes it at row 16. The result is that the current row 16 is moved downward and the copy placed at the desired row.

```
ActiveCell.EntireRow.Copy
Range("A16").Insert
```

Finally, you can also use the PasteSpecial method to paste information previously copied to the Clipboard. (I don't know about you, but I use Excel's Paste Special feature quite a bit in my work.) To understand what the PasteSpecial method does, it may be helpful to take a quick peek at the Paste Special dialog box in Excel (see Figure 11-3).

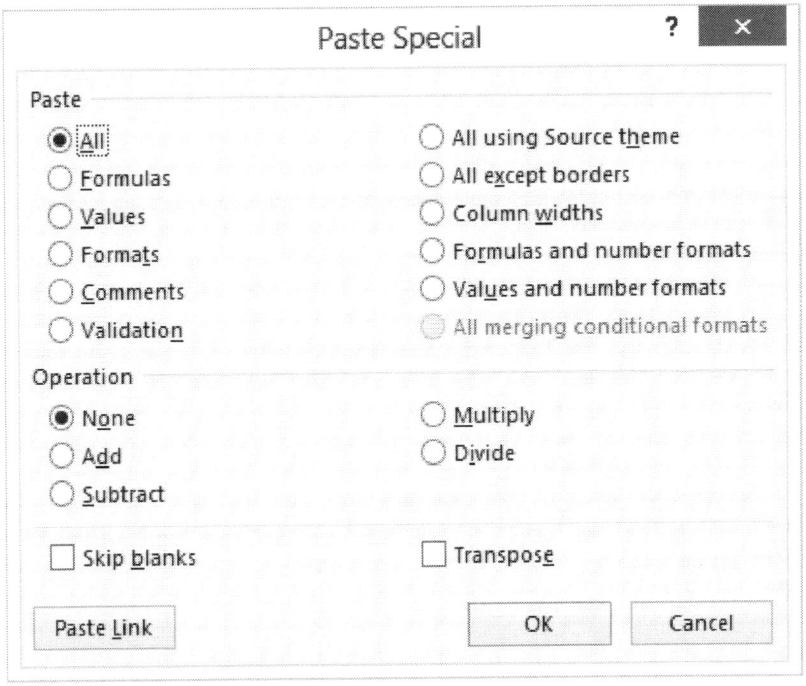

Figure 11-3. Excel's Paste Special dialog box is very powerful.

Each of the radio buttons in the Paste Special dialog box implements a different way of pasting the information that is in the Clipboard. In order to use the PasteSpecial method in VBA, you need to use the following structure when putting together the code for the PasteSpecial method:

```
objRange.PasteSpecial(Paste, Operation, SkipBlanks, Transpose)
```

All of the parameters between the parentheses are optional, but each of them allows you to perform any of the pasting operations you'd normally do using the Paste Special dialog box. You can, if you look closely enough at the dialog box, figure out what each of the four parameters means—*Paste* means a setting that that matches up with the Paste section of the dialog box, *Operation* with the Operation section, and the final two with the two check boxes.

Here's the enumerations you can use to designate how you want your information pasted. (Use one of these for the *Paste* parameter.) I've placed these in the same order they appear in the Paste Special dialog box, top to bottom and left to right:

- xlPasteAll
- xlPasteFormulas
- xlPasteValues
- xlPasteFormats
- xlPasteComments
- xlPasteValidation
- xlPasteAllUsingSourceTheme
- xlPasteAllExceptBorders
- xlPasteColumnWidths
- xlPasteFormulasAndNumberFormats
- xlPasteValuesAndNumberFormats
- xlPasteAllMergingConditionalFormats

Here's the enumerations you can use for the operation you want performed by the PasteSpecial method. (Use one of these for the *Operation* parameter.) Again, these are in the same order they appear in the Paste Special dialog box:

- xlPasteSpecialOperationNone
- xlPasteSpecialOperationAdd
- xlPasteSpecialOperationSubtract
- xlPasteSpecialOperationMultiply
- xlPasteSpecialOperationDivide

Finally, here's some sample code that shows how you can copy information from one area and paste the values into another area:

```
Range("A2:A49").Copy
Range("J2").PasteSpecial Paste:=xlPasteValues
```

Setting Row Height and Column Width

As part of your processing of a worksheet, you may be interested in changing the height of a row using a macro. If so, you should pay attention to the

RowHeight property. This property, when applied to a Row object, indicates the height of the row in points.

For instance, the following code steps through the rows in a selection and sets the height of each row to 36 points (one-half inch):

```
Dim r As Range

For Each r In Selection.Rows
    r.RowHeight = 36
Next r
```

Setting column width is just as easy—you just need to use the ColumnWidth property. This property, when applied to a Column object, indicates the width of the column in characters, based on the current font settings.

For instance, the following code steps through the columns in a selection and sets the width of each column to 10 characters:

```
Dim c As Range

For Each c In Selection.Columns
    c.ColumnWidth = 10
Next c
```

12

Working with Workbooks

At the heart of everything that Excel does is the workbook. We tend to take workbooks for granted, but everything created in Excel is contained within one. Because they are at the heart of Excel, they are also at the heart of working with VBA in Excel. In this chapter you'll discover all sorts of things about workbooks:

- Ways to work with the Workbook object
- How to create new workbooks
- How to open an existing workbook
- How to work with specific workbooks (when you have multiple ones open)
- Saving information in a workbook

The Workbook Object

A Workbook object represents, well, a single workbook open in Excel at the current time. Each Workbook object is part of the Workbooks collection. Excel allows you to have open, at any given time, any number of workbooks, so the Workbooks collection can contain any number of Workbook objects.

Individual Workbook objects can be accessed within two ways. First, you can access them by index or by name within the Workbooks collection; this access method is no different than any other collection you may work with. This means that you can use a loop to step through the collection and access each Workbook's information, like this:

```
Dim w As Workbook
Dim sWBNames(99) As String
Dim iWBptr As Integer

iWBptr = 0
For Each w in Workbooks
    iWBptr = iWBptr + 1
    sWBNames(iWBptr) = w.Name
Next w
```

When this code is through, the sWBNames array contains the names of all the workbooks currently open in Excel. (You'll learn more about workbook names later in this chapter.) The key here is to notice how easy it is to access information about the individual workbooks simply by accessing each member of the Workbooks collection. You'll find more detail about accessing individual Workbook objects later in this chapter.

The second way to access an individual Workbook object is with the special ActiveWorkbook object. This object is synonymous with whichever workbook currently is active (has focus) in Excel. The actual Workbook object to which it refers changes as the selected workbook changes. It is a very handy object, one that you'll use many times in your macros.

There are scores of methods and properties that belong to Workbook objects, but only a few of them are key to successfully working with that object.

Creating New Workbooks

It is often necessary to create new workbooks in a macro. Perhaps you need to create some information and you don't want that information to be inserted in an existing workbook. The answer is to use the Add method with the Workbooks collection:

```
Workbooks.Add
```

This usage creates a new workbook and adds the Workbook object to the Workbooks collection. When you add a new workbook, you now have a minimum of two workbooks open in Excel—the one that existed when you ran your macro and the one you just added. Because of this, it is helpful to be able to keep track of which workbook you are working with in your macro.

A common technique for doing this is to assign the Workbook object to your own object variables. Consider the following code:

```
Dim wbThis As Workbook
Dim wbThat As Workbook

Set wbThis = ActiveWorkbook
Workbooks.Add
Set wbThat = ActiveWorkbook
wbThis.Activate
```

Note that the Set keyword, discussed in Chapter 2, is used to make the wbThis variable equal to the ActiveWorkbook object. The ActiveWorkbook object is a special instance of whatever workbook Excel considers active at the current time; it is whatever workbook currently has the focus.

The code then uses the Add method to add a workbook, just as you learned. When this occurs, the new workbook then has focus as far as Excel is concerned. That is why the next line sets the wbThat variable equal to the ActiveWorkbook. The final line activates the original workbook, represented by the wbThis variable.

What you end up with when executing this code is wbThis being equivalent to the first workbook and wbThat being equivalent to the newly added workbook. You can then reference each workbook in your code directly using the object variables, wbThis and wbThat.

Opening Existing Workbooks

If your macro needs to open an existing workbook, you use the Open method with the Workbooks collection. If the method is successful in opening the workbook, then a Workbook object is added to the collection and refers to the workbook you opened.

Here is the simplest way to open a workbook:

```
Workbooks.Open("c:/mydata/myworkbook.xlsx")
```

The important thing to keep in mind here is that in order to be unambiguous the filename must include the full path to the workbook. If you don't include the full path, there is a greater chance that VBA won't be successful in opening the file because you never really know what directory the program considers the current directory.

In all of its glory, the Open method allows you to specify up to 15 parameters. All of these are optional, with the exception of the first parameter, the filename. To use other parameters, simply include them with the Open method's parentheses, right after the filename. Just separate the parameters with commas. The other 14 parameters are as follows, in order:

- **UpdateLinks.** Specifies the way external links in the workbook are updated. Set to 0 to stop the links from being updated or 3 to have Excel update them.

- **ReadOnly.** True or False, depending on whether you want the workbook opened as read-only or not.

- **Format.** Only has meaning when opening a text file. Used to indicate what character should be used as a delimiter in the imported information. Set to 1 (tabs), 2 (commas), 3 (spaces), 4 (semicolons), 5 (nothing), or 6 (use what is specified in the Delimiter parameter).

- **Password.** The workbook's password.

- **WriteResPassword.** The password for saving workbook changes, if the workbook was saved using a write-reserve setting.

- **IgnoreReadOnlyRecommended.** True or False, depending on whether you want Excel to display the read-only recommended message. (Only has meaning if the workbook was saved with the read-only recommended setting.)

- **Origin.** Only has meaning when opening a text file. Used to indicate the source of the data: Windows (xlWindows), DOS (xlMSDOS), or Macintosh (xlMacintosh).

- **Delimiter.** Used in conjunction with the Format parameter to specify the delimiter character in a text file.

- **Editable.** This setting is meaningless in modern versions of Excel.

- **Notify.** True or False, depending on whether you want the user notified if Excel has problems opening the workbook when it is already opened by another.

- **Converter.** An indicator (index value) that specifies which file converter to use whe opening the file.

- **AddToMru.**True orFalse, depending on whether you want the file added to the MRU list in Excel. (The default value is False.)

- **Local.** True or False, depending on whether the file should be analyzed against the local users' language or against the default language (US English) used for VBA.

- **CorruptLoad.** Specifies what Excel should do if it detects the file being opened is corrupted in some way. Can be set to xlNormalLoad (the default), xlRepairFile, or xlExtractData.

Of course, most of these parameters you would never use in opening a plain old Excel workbook. In most cases you can get by just fine with using just the filename and its path.

Getting to a Workbook's Name

One of the properties associated with a workbook allows you to determine what its name is. This is handy when you are working with whatever workbook the user opened before your macro started running.

In reality, there are three properties that are related to names:

- **Name.** Returns the name of the workbook, meaning the filename the workbook uses when saved on disk. If the workbook has yet to be saved, then a placeholder name (such as Book1 or Book2) is returned.

- **FullName.** Returns the full path and filename for the workbook. If the workbook has yet to be saved, then this property returns the same as the Name property.

- **Path.** Returns the full path to the folder in which the filename is stored, without a trailing slash.

In looking at the properties related to workbook names, you may wonder how you can really tell whether a workbook has been previously saved or not. You'll note that the Name property returns a placeholder name if the workbook has not been saved, but there is nothing to stop the user from saving a workbook using that placeholder name.

The technique to use is to compare the Name property to the FullName property. If they are the same, then the workbook has never been saved:

```
Dim bSavedBefore As Boolean

bSavedBefore = True
With ActiveWorkbook
    If .Name = .FullName Then bSavedBefore = False
End With
If bSavedBefore Then
    MsgBox "Workbook has been saved before."
Else
    MsgBox "Workbook has not been saved yet."
End If
```

Accessing Workbooks

Since Excel stores all its data in workbooks, it is critical that you understand how to access those workbooks within your programming code. The following sections detail how you can get right to the workbook you need.

Working with Specific Workbooks

When you are working with multiple workbooks open at the same time, it is normal to assign each workbook to its own Workbook object, thereby making accessing the workbook easier. Remember, though, that whenever you create a Workbook object (whether by adding a new workbook or opening an existing workbook), that object is added to the Workbooks collection. This means that you can easily access the individual workbooks by number, as in this manner:

```
Dim wbTarget As Workbook

Set wbTarget = Workbooks(2)
```

This code sets the wbTarget variable so that it references the second Workbook object in the Workbooks collection. The problem is, Workbook objects are not stored in the Workbooks collection in any particular order. Generally, people expect the order to be the order in which workbooks are opened, but when you start opening and closing a lot of workbooks in the same session, then the order can quickly start to appear capricious.

Generally, you should only rely on index numbers when you need to step through the Workbooks collection in some way. For instance, you may want to step through the collection in order to determine the name of each workbook. Here is one way to accomplish the task:

```
Dim sTemp As String
Dim J As Integer

sTemp = "Here are the workbooks currently open:" & vbCrLf & vbCrLf
For J = 1 To Workbooks.Count
    sTemp = sTemp & "    " & Workbooks(J).Name & vbCrLf
Next J

MsgBox sTemp
```

There is, of course, another way that you could accomplish the same task without even worrying about the index number, however:

```
Dim wb As Workbook
Dim sTemp As String

sTemp = "Here are the workbooks currently open:" & vbCrLf & vbCrLf
For Each wb in Workbooks
    sTemp = sTemp & "    " & wb.Name & vbCrLf
Next wb

MsgBox sTemp
```

If you need to specify a specific Workbook object, the best way is to use the workbook's name as the index into the Workbooks collection. The name should be easy to get, particularly if you used the Open method to open the workbook within your code. All you need to do is make sure that you provide the name for the workbook in place of the index number:

```
Dim wbTarget As Workbook

Set wbTarget = Workbooks("2014 Budget.xlsx")
```

Note that you don't need to use the full path name with this technique; just use the filename and extension.

You should also note that workbooks don't really have filenames and extensions until you save them to disk. Therefore, this method of referencing a specific workbook should not be used for workbooks that are brand new, before they are saved to disk.

Activating Workbooks

When you have multiple workbooks open at once, not only do you need to worry about making sure you are referencing the right workbook (as detailed in the preceding section), you also need to worry about which workbook is active at the current time.

A workbook is said to be active when it is visible and has focus. When you are working in a workbook (not using a macro, but working directly in a workbook), a single workbook is active and you can switch which workbook is active by simple clicking somewhere within a workbook.

Obviously, you cannot "click" using a macro. You can, however, give a workbook "focus" by using the Activate method, in this manner:

```
wbTarget.Activate
```

This usage assumes that you previously set the wbTarget variable to reference a Workbook object. You generally need to activate a workbook before you can use macro commands to make any changes in that workbook.

Saving Workbooks

VBA provides three different methods you can use to save your workbook: Close, Save, and SaveAs. Each of these is detailed in the following sections.

The Close Method

When you are done processing a workbook in your macro, chances are good that you'll want to close it. This is done by using the Close method, in this manner:

```
ActiveWorkbook.Close
```

Of course, you can use a different Workbook object in place of the ActiveWorkbook object. The Close method prompts you to save your changes (if necessary) and then closes the workbook. If you want to close the workbook without being prompted about saving changes, you can use the following:

```
ActiveWorkbook.Close(False)
```

This results in the changes not being saved; they are discarded. If you would rather simply have any changes saved without being prompted, then you should use the following:

```
ActiveWorkbook.Close(True)
```

If you want your changes saved in a different filename than the current one, then you can add a comma and a full filename to the parameters used with the Close method:

```
ActiveWorkbook.Close(True, "c:/mydata/newplace.xlsx")
```

When you specify a filename with the Close method, it works very similarly to the SaveAs method, as described shortly.

Interestingly, you can use the Close method with the entire Workbooks collection. This results in all the currently open workbooks being saved. In this case you would use this command:

```
Workbooks.Close
```

The Save Method

As you are working with a workbook, it is good practice to periodically save your changes. This prevents a catastrophe in case your system crashes for some reason. The Save method is the same as clicking the Save icon on the Quick Access Toolbar (the one that looks like a small diskette).

```
ActiveWorkbook.Save
```

If the workbook being saved has not been previously saved, then Excel displays the Save As dialog box, described in the next section.

When you are done using the Save method, the workbook that was saved is still open in Excel. You can do additional processing from that point, or you can close the workbook as discussed in the previous section.

The SaveAs Method

If you want to save a workbook using a new name or in a different format, you'll typically use the SaveAs method. There are a myriad of parameters you can use with the SaveAs method, but this is typically the bare minimum:

```
ActiveWorkbook.SaveAs("c:/mydata/mynewworkbook.xlsx")
```

If you want to set the other parameters available with the SaveAs method, simply add them within the parentheses and separate them by commas. The additional parameters are as follows, in order:

- **FileFormat.** A numeric indicator of what file format should be used for the saved workbook. This indicator seems to change from version to version of Excel; check the online help for information on what codes can be used.

- **Password.** A password subsequently required to open the workbook.

- **WriteResPassword.** If supplied, then Excel saves the workbook as "write reserved." This password must be supplied when opening the workbook in the future, or Excel opens it as read-only.

- **ReadOnlyRecommended.** True or False, signifying whether you want a warning displayed when the workbook is later opened. (The warning would tell the user that the workbook should be saved under a different name.)

- **CreateBackup.** True or False, signifying whether you want Excel to save a backup of the workbook.

- **AccessMode.** The access mode for the workbook. (Sounds cryptic, huh? See online help for more information about this parameter.)

- **ConflictResolution.** A value that determines how Excel resolves any conflict that arrises when saving the workbook. Can be set to xlUserResolution (the user is asked in a dialog box how to resolve the conflict), xlLocalSessionChanges (the user's changes are automatically accepted), or xlOtherSessionChanges (the changes from other sessions take precedence over the user's changes).

- **AddToMru.** True or False, signifyinig whether the workbook should be added to the MRU list or not. (The default is False.)

- **TextCodepage.** Only comes into play when saving in CSV or text format. Used to signify which coding "format" to use in the saved file. (This parameter is ignored in the latest versions of Excel.)

- **TextVisualLayout.** Only comes into play when saving in CSV or text format. Used to signify which "direction" should be used in saving the data in the workbook. (This parameter is ignored in the latest versions of Excel.)

- **Local.** True or False, signifying whether the workbook should be saved using the user's local language or the default language used for VBA (US English).

Unless you want to actually set each of the parameters under program control, it is usually a good idea to simply use the Save method, instead of the SaveAs method, and allow the user to specify all the parameters in the Save As dialog box.

The SaveAs method is similar in results to the Save method, in that when you are done using it the workbook that was saved is still open in Excel.

13

Searching and Replacing

One of the most powerful editing tools that Excel provides is the Find and Replace tool. This tool can be just as powerful when you are using it under the control of your macros. The only thing you need to master when it comes to finding things is the Find object. Secondary to the Find object is the Replacement object, which allows you to replace whatever you are able to find.

This chapter focuses on the ways you can use Find and Replace within your macro code. When you are done you'll be able to whip through a find and replace in no time.

Finding Things

At the root of using Find and Replace within your macro is the Find object. The easiest way to see how Excel puts this object together is to record a macro that looks for something simple. For instance, let's say that you work for Imperial Widget Company and you want to search for instances of the word *Widget* in your worksheet. Perform these steps:

1. Display the Developer tab of the ribbon.
2. Click the Record Macro tool. Excel displays the Record Macro dialog box, as shown in Figure 13-1.
3. Click OK. Excel starts the recording process.
4. Press **CTRL+F**. Excel displays the Find tab of the Find and Replace dialog box, shown in Figure 13-2.

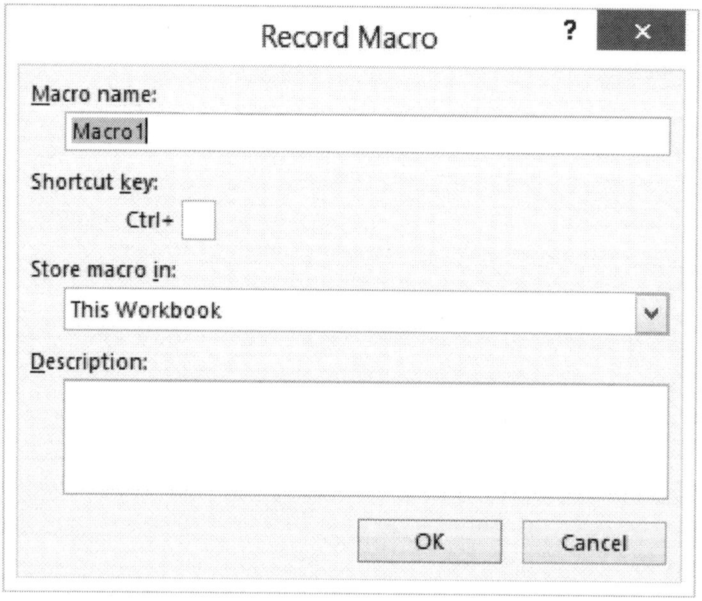

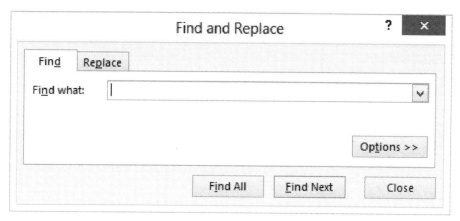

Figure 13-1. *Getting ready to record a macro.*

Figure 13-2. *Searching for something in Excel.*

5. In the Find What box, enter the word **Widget**.

6. Click Find Next.

7. Press **Esc** to dismiss the Find and Replace dialog box.

8. Click Stop Recording.

If you take a look at the code generated by the macro recorder, you'll see that it looks very similar to this:

```
Sub Macro1()
'
' Macro1 Macro
'

'
    Cells.Find(What:="Widget", After:=ActiveCell, LookIn:=xlFormulas, LookAt
_
        :=xlPart, SearchOrder:=xlByRows, SearchDirection:=xlNext,
MatchCase:= _
        False, SearchFormat:=False).Activate
End Sub
```

Note the use of the Find method, which makes up the bulk of this macro's single command line. This method works with any Range object. In the case of this recorded macro, it is used with the Cells object, which is the range of all cells in the worksheet. Examining how Excel performs this find operation is instructive, and understanding what is going on can help you tap into the real power behind searching for information.

Find Parameters

The bulk of the recorded macro shown in the previous section dealt with setting parameters. These parameters define exactly how the Find method is to actually do its searching. Here are the parameters you are most likely to use; you'll notice several from this list were used by Excel in the recorded macro.

- **What.** The text or value you want to locate.
- **After.** The single cell after which you want the search to begin. When recording a macro, the After parameter is always set to the ActiveCell range, but you can set it to any cell you desire. If you don't specify the After parameter, then Excel starts the search at the upper-left corner of the range. The search begins after this cell, which means that the After cell itself isn't searched until the Find method wraps back around to the cell.
- **LookIn.** Specifies what should be searched within the range: xlFormulas, xlValues, or xlComments.
- **LookAt.** Specifies the granularity of the search. You can specify for Excel to look at xlWhole (entire cells) or xlPart (portions of cells).

- **SearchOrder.** Specifies the orientation of the search: xlByRows or xlByColumns.

- **SearchDirection.** Specifies the direction of the search: xlNext (next match) or xlPrevious (previous match).

- **MatchCase.** True or False, indicating if the search should be sensitive to letter case.

- **SearchFormat.** The format of what you want to find. Normally set to False if you don't care about the format of what you are searching for.

You should understand that the parameters are somewhat persistent in nature. In other words, if you do a search and set some of the parameters (either manually or using a macro), then the next time you do a search those parameters are still set. Thus, it is a good idea to make sure you always completely set whatever parameters you need for your search.

Searching and Searching

Note that when the Find method is complete, what is returned is a Range object that represents the first cell that matches whatever you are searching for. Thus, Find always returns a single cell, provided a match was located. If no match was located, then the Find method returns nothing.

Once you've conducted a search, you can search for the same thing again by using either the FindNext or FindPrevious method. As you might infer from their names, the FindNext method returns a Range object for the next cell that matches your criteria, while the FindPrevious does the opposite and returns a Range object for the previous matching cell.

Interestingly (and potentially problematic), the Find method is rather circular in its operation. Remember that Excel always does its searching from a starting cell, specified in the After parameter. The next time you search (whether it is using Find, FindNext, or FindPrevious) without specifying a new After parameter, Excel starts the search from where the previous search left off. When the end of the range being searched is encountered, the searching starts over again at the beginning of the range.

The potential problem crops up when you keep cycling through the range, over and over again. Excel doesn't signal "Hey! I've found this particular cell before," nor does it tell you it is through searching the range you designated. It is up to you to keep track of where you started and figure out if you've been through the entire range once. Most of the time you do this by doing your initial search, but keeping track of how you set the After parameter. If any cell found is before this parameter, then you know that a complete cycle hasn't occurred. If any cell found is after this parameter, then it is possible you've cycled through the range at least once. If you keep track of the first matching cell found, and what is subsequently found matches that cell again, then you know you've been through the entire cycle.

This method of searching a range is a bit rudimentary; Excel isn't terribly helpful in letting you know what you've done before. For this reason, you may want to do what many people do in their macros—forego using the Find method and, instead, simply step through each cell in the desired range to see if your criteria are met. Stepping through cells is easier, albeit not quite as quick as using the Find method (particularly if you are working with many, many cells.)

Searching Multiple Worksheets

The Find method works on the active worksheet. If you want to search more than one worksheet in the current workbook, you need to do your searching on one worksheet, then switch to another worksheet and search there. Searching is done, one worksheet after another, until you are through with all the worksheets you wanted to search.

As an example, lets expand a bit on the widget example used earlier in this chapter. If you want to search all the worksheets in the workbook for instances of the word *widget,* you could use code like this:

```
Sub FindAcrossAll()
    Dim s As Worksheet
    Dim DoIt As Boolean
    Dim Msg As String
    Dim Style As Long
    Dim Title As String
    Dim Response As Long
    Dim FindWhat As String
    Dim Found As Range
    Dim FirstAddress As String
```

```
            DoIt = True
            While DoIt
                FindWhat = "widget"
                For Each s In Worksheets
                    s.Activate
                    Set Found = s.UsedRange.Find(What:=FindWhat, _
                        LookIn:=xlFormulas, LookAt:=xlPart, _
                        SearchOrder:=xlByRows, SearchDirection:=xlNext, _
                        MatchCase:=False, SearchFormat:=False)
                    If Not Found Is Nothing Then      ' The value has been found
                        FirstAddress = Found.Address
                        Do
                            Found.Activate
                            Msg = "Continue searching?"
                            Title = "Continue?"
                            Response = MsgBox(Msg, vbYesNo + vbQuestion, Title)
                            If Response = vbNo Then Exit Sub   'All done
                            Set Found = Cells.FindNext(After:=ActiveCell)
                            If Found.Address = FirstAddress Then Exit Do
                        Loop
                    End If
                Next s
                If Found Is Nothing Then         ' Nothing found
                    Msg = "Not found! Start a new search?"
                    Style = vbYesNo + vbCritical + vbDefaultButton2
                Else
                    Msg = "Search complete. Start a new search?"
                    Style = vbYesNo + vbDefaultButton2
                End If
                Title = "Search Complete"
                Response = MsgBox(Msg, Style, Title)
                If Response <> vbYes Then DoIt = False
            Wend
            MsgBox ("Search is complete")
        End Sub
```

Granted, you don't have to use code like this to find instances of a term across worksheets; Excel's user interface for Find and Replace will search multiple worksheets just fine. What the code shows, however, is how you could step through worksheets to look for a value. What you do with that value once you find it is up to you and your imagination.

Using Find to Modify Your Worksheet

You know that you can use Find and Replace to modify the contents of your worksheets. How you do that is detailed a bit later in this chapter. However, your macro can greatly modify what is in your worksheet in ways that a simple Find and Replace could never do.

The idea is to search for something and then, each time it is found, edit the value in some way that fits your needs. As an example, let's say that you have a worksheet in which there are a series of formulas that rely on a named value called "Markup." You want to modify each of these formulas to make sure that instead of the Markup value you use a value named "NewMark." Further, you then wanted to make sure that those changed cells were formatted as bold. You could do that in this way:

```
Sub ChangeMarkup()
    Dim MyRange As Range
    Dim Found As Range
    Dim sTemp As String

    Set MyRange = Cells.SpecialCells(xlCellTypeFormulas)
    Set Found = MyRange.Find("Markup", LookIn:=xlFormulas, _
      LookAt:=xlPart, MatchCase:=True)
    While Not Found Is Nothing
        sTemp = Found.Formula
        sTemp = Replace(sTemp, "Markup", "NewMark")
        Found.Formula = sTemp
        Found.Font.Bold = True
        Set Found = MyRange.FindNext
    Wend
End Sub
```

Note that this routine starts by setting what you want to search—only those cells in the worksheet that contain formulas. (You don't want to modify any instances of the word *Markup* anywhere except in formulas.) This is done by setting the MyRange object to contain only the cells that contain formulas. This object (MyRange) is then used with the Find method to locate the cells that contain the Markup name. This is changed to NewMark, stuffed back into the cell's formula, and then the cell is set as bold.

Even in a very large worksheet, this macro runs almost instantaneously, and the formulas and formatting are all chaged as desired. If you need to make changes like this in a lot of worksheets, the time savings can be immeasurable.

Replacing Things

When it comes time to do simple replacements in a worksheet, you can rely on the Replace method. The method works in much the same way as the Find method, as it relies on many of the same parameters. For the sake of clarity, however, Replace uses these parameters:

- **What.** The text or value you want to locate.

- **Replacement.** The text or value you want to replace the What parameter with.

- **LookAt.** Specifies the granularity of the search. You can specify for Excel to look at xlWhole (entire cells) or xlPart (portions of cells).

- **SearchOrder.** Specifies the orientation of the search: xlByRows or xlByColumns.

- **MatchCase.** True or False, indicating if the search should be sensitive to letter case.

- **SearchFormat.** The format of what you want to find. Normally set to False if you don't care about the format of what you are searching for.

- **ReplaceFormat.** The format you want to use for the replacement.

As an example, let's say you wanted to replace all instances of the word *Company* with the word *Corporation*. You could do that by using the Replace method in this manner:

```
Cells.Replace(What:="Company", Replacement:="Corporation", _
    LookAt:=xlPart, SearchOrder:=xlByRows, MatchCase:=True)
```

You should note that the Replace method is significantly different than the Find method in that it doesn't return a Range object that represents a cell. Instead it returns either True or False, depending on whether there were any replacements made or not.

The Replace method also doesn't ask you if you want to make the changes you are trying to make—if it finds a match, then the replacement is immediately made.

Searching and Replacing Formatting

Excel provides two objects which are used whenever you want to search for or replace formatting: FindFormat and ReplaceFormat. These objects are members of the Application object. You define the characteristics of the objects by setting their properties, and then you can use the Find or Replace methods, as outlined earlier in this chapter, to do the actual searching or replacing.

Let's say that you want to replace all the cells that are explicitly right-aligned so they are, instead, left-aligned. You can do that using the following code:

```
With Application.FindFormat
    .Clear
    .HoizontalAlignment = xlRight
End With

With Application.ReplaceFormat
    .Clear
    .HorizontalAlignment = xlLeft
End With

Cells.Replace(SearchFormat:=True, ReplaceFormat:=True)
```

Note that the Find method has a SearchFormat parameter, as does the Replace method. In addition, the Replace method also has a ReplaceFormat parameter. These parameters can be either True or False. If you don't care about formatting, then these parameters are set to False. If you do care about formatting, then you set them to True.

If the SearchFormat parameter is True, then Excel uses the FindFormat object as a definition of what formatting should be used in the search. Similarly, if the ReplaceFormat parameter is True, then Excel uses the ReplaceFormat object as a definition of the replacement formatting it should use.

When you are setting up definitions for either the FindFormat or ReplaceFormat objects, it s a good idea to "clear the slate" before you set properties. You can see this done in the code just provided; the Clear method is used to set everything back to default. You can then, with both the FindFormat and ReplaceFormat objects, have any of the following properties specified:

- AddIndent
- Borders
- Font
- FormulaHidden
- HorizontalAlignment
- IndentLevel
- Interior
- Locked
- MergeCells
- NumberFormat
- NumberFormatLocal
- Orientation
- ShrinkToFit
- VerticalAlignment
- WrapText

Each of these properties can be set using built-in enumeration values. These potential values are quite extensive and can be located in the online VBA help. Some of the properties reference, in turn, their own objects which can have additional properties. This is especially true with the Font property, which can have an extensive number of additional properties you can specify.

14

Worksheet and User-Defined Functions

In Chapter 2 you discovered that one of the types of procedures you can create in VBA is referred to as a function. Functions, as described there, are integral to working efficiently in VBA. However, in Excel's implementation of VBA there are some additional types of functions you need to know about: Worksheet functions and user-defined functions. This chapter covers both of these powerful topics.

Accessing Worksheet Functions

If you've been using Excel for any length of time, you know that the power behind the your worksheets is the functions that Excel makes available. Covering everything from working with text to doing trigonometric and financial calculations, worksheet functions provide a vast range of functionality to your formulas.

Rather than re-invent the wheel in VBA, you can access virtually any worksheet function you want within your code. It's easy to do using the WorksheetFunction property, which is a member of the Application object. For example, here's how you could use the SUM function within your macro:

```
Dim MyRange As Range
Dim MyResult As Double
```

```
Set MyRange = Range("A1:A100")
MyResult = WorksheetFunction.Sum(MyRange)
```

This is very similar to how you would use the SUM function within the worksheet itself:

```
=SUM(A1:A100)
```

The WorksheetFunction property allows you to access hundreds and hundreds of worksheet functions (actually over 600 functions, and counting). You use those functions, in VBA, in almost the same way you use them in an Excel worksheet.

Excel does provide some worksheet functions that essentially duplicate things you can already do in VBA, natively. For instance, the LEFT worksheet function allows you to grab the left-most characters of a string. In VBA there is, similarly, a Left function that does the same thing. In those instances where there is apparent duplication, then the worksheet function that would duplicate what VBA can do is not made available through the WorksheetFunction property— there is no need.

Creating User-Defined Functions

In VBA, a function is used to perform some operation and then return a value to whatever programming code called that function. For instance, the following is a simple function you can use to return the first character from a string:

```
Function FirstChar(sRaw As String) As String
    FirstChar = Left(sRaw, 1)
End Function
```

To use the function, all you need to do is pass it the string you want to work on:

```
sMyFirst = FirstChar(sLongString)
```

When done, the sMyFirst variable will contain the first character of whatever is in the sLongString variable.

If you want, you can create your functions so that they are accessible not just from other VBA code, but also from within a worksheet. Functions designed for this purpose are often called *user-defined functions*, or (for short) UDFs. The terminology can get a bit confusing, as technically all functions you create in VBA are user-defined (you are the user, after all). It would be more technically correct to refer to a function designed to return information to your worksheet as a user-defined worksheet function.

The trick to creating your own UDFs is to determine what single piece of information you want that function to return, along with what pieces of information you need to provide to it. For example, let's say you needed to routinely determine the number of uppercase "R" characters there are in a range of cells. What you need back is a count (a number) and what you need to supply is the range of cells to check. Here's the macro you might come up with:

```
Function NumRs(rng As Range) As Integer
    Dim iCnt As Integer
    Dim c As Range
    Dim sTemp As String
    Dim J As Integer

    iCnt = 0
    For Each c In rng.Cells
        sTemp = c.Value
        For J = 1 To Len(sTemp)
            If Mid(sTemp, J, 1) = "B" Then iCnt = iCnt + 1
        Next J
    Next c
    NumRs = iCnt
End Function
```

Note that UDFs are very similar in structure to regular VBA function—you pass a value (or values) to the UDF and it passes a value back. To use the function, you would use a formula like this in your worksheet:

```
=NumRs(B3:H3)
```

The function returns the number of uppercase "R" characters in the range B3:H3. The result that is stuffed into the cell is accessible by any other formula within your worksheet.

Running Your UDF whenever the Worksheet is Recalculated

When you write a function in VBA, it is designed to be run whenever you choose to run it—in other words, whenever it is invoked from some other piece of code. When you work with UDFs, they are invoked when you first enter them into a cell. You probably, however, want them to be run whenever you recalculate your worksheet. This is particularly true if your UDF relies upon information in the worksheet itself—information that may change.

This is where the Volatile method comes in handy. All you need to do is include the following statement within your macro:

```
Application.Volatile
```

This informs Excel that the results of the macro are dependent on the values in the worksheet, and that it should be executed whenever the worksheet is recalculated. Note that the macro is executed every time any cell in the worksheet is recalculated. If you can avoid using the statement, then you should do so—it will slow down your recalculations. That being said, there are times when it is proper to use it.

How do you know when you should use it? Perhaps an example or two will help. First, consider the following short user-defined function:

```
Function CountCells(MyRange As Range)
    Dim iCount As Integer
    iCount = 0
    For Each cell In MyRange
        If cell.HasFormula Then
            iCount = iCount + 1
        End If
    Next cell
    CountCells = iCount
End Function
```

This function, if used in a cell, counts the number of cells that contain formulas within a specified range. Since you are passing a range to the function, Excel knows the cells on which the function relies. That means that anytime a cell within that range changes, Excel knows that it should again execute the macro because the cells on which it depends have changed. This is great; you'll always get the result you expect from your function.

However, you might have a macro that depends on cells in the worksheet and for which the address is not passed in the function call. Let's rewrite that CountCells macro just a bit to show what this means:

```
Function CountCells()
    Dim iCount As Integer
    Dim MyRange As Range

    iCount = 0
    Set MyRange = Cells.Range("B4:B12")
    For Each cell In MyRange
        If cell.HasFormula Then
            iCount = iCount + 1
        End If
    Next cell
    CountCells = iCount
End Function
```

Note that no range address is passed to this function; it is hard-coded to use the range B4:B12. When you first enter this function into a cell, Excel executes it and it returns the expected result. It is also run whenever the cell containing the function call is edited. It is not run, however, whenever something in the range B4:B12 is changed, even though the function depends upon values in that range.

The solution in this instance—when your macro directly accesses worksheet values and depends on them—is to add the Volatile method near the beginning of the function:

```
Function CountCells()
    Dim iCount As Integer
    Dim MyRange As Range

    Application.Volatile
    iCount = 0
    Set MyRange = Cells.Range("B4:B12")
    For Each cell In MyRange
        If cell.HasFormula Then
            iCount = iCount + 1
        End If
    Next cell
    CountCells = iCount
End Function
```

The inclusion of the Application.Volatile method means that every time the worksheet is recalculated, for whatever reason, this function (macro) is again run.

Making Sure a Function Isn't Used as a UDF

When you create a function as discussed in these foregoing sections, Excel automatically assumes you can use it from the worksheet itself. You can see this by following these steps:

1. Display the Formulas tab of the ribbon.

2. Click the Insert Function tool, at the left side of the ribbon. Excel displays the Insert Function dialog box.

3. Using the Select a Category drop-down list, choose User Defined. (This option is available only if you've defined any UDFs.) The dialog box appears as shown in Figure 14-1.

However, you may have a function or number of functions that you don't want used as UDFs, for some reason. Perhaps they are designed to specifically work only with specific macros, or perhaps you don't want them to be generally available from within a worksheet. Whatever the reason, you need a way to keep them private.

As you discovered in Chapter 2, you can control the scope of the VBA procedures you create. If you don't want your function to be widely used, then precede the function declaration with the Private keyword, in this manner:

```
Private MyUDF(rng As Range, c As Integer) As Boolean
```

The inclusion on the Private keyword informs Excel that you don't want the function available from anywhere other than the module in which it is defined. This includes in the Insert Function dialog box.

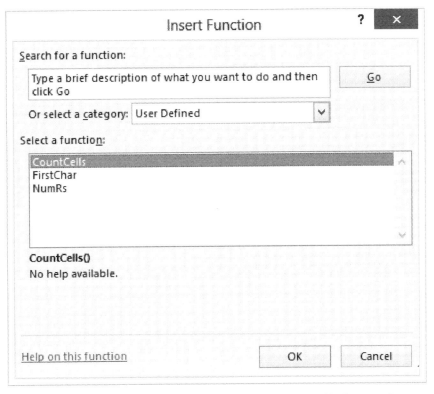

Figure 14-1. Your user-defined functions are available from within Excel's user interface.

15

Working with Non-Excel Files

All the VBA programs you have created thus far have accessed information entered by an end user or existing within an Excel workbook. Although this may be sufficient for some macros, it is inevitable that you'll need to read data from or write data to a disk file.

Unless you use data files, your programs will never be able to remember what the user of the program did the last time they ran the program. Data files are used to store information so the information can be retrieved at some time in the future when you again run your VBA program.

Sometimes files are used to store configuration information such as the user's name and their preferred options. Other times, files are used to remember aspects such as the last invoice number used or the last date a macro was used. Other times, data files are used to store database information such as data about customers and orders. All these reasons and many more are valid reasons to create and use your own data files in a VBA macro.

In this chapter, you'll uncover the types of data files that you may need to access from within a macro and cover how to do so using VBA.

File Types

Files are used for a wide variety of purposes on computers. Almost every commercial program, including Excel, uses files in one way or another. These programs create and maintain files with information for their own use or to share with other programs.

There are numerous types of files that you can have on your computer. Typically the file's extension (the portion of the filename after the period) identifies what type of file it is, although nothing forces this identification except tradition.

Although each file extension typically identifies the file type, most file types are only understood by the programs that use them. Windows does not know one type of file from the next—at least not from the filename alone. Typically, Windows only sees a file as being a series of characters that can be interpreted in any number of ways. The format of a file is usually determined by the program that uses it.

Although Windows does not typically care about specific types of files, there are different formats that can be used by and are used by various programs. You need to read and update each of these formats differently. The remainder of this section discusses these different kinds of formats:

- Text files
- Foreign file formats
- Import/Export formats
- Initialization (.INI) files
- Simple multiple record databases.

Text Files

ASCII stands for American Standard Code for Information Interchange and it defines standard characters for interchanging information on a computer. In ASCII, each character is assigned a numeric code that is used to represent and store that character in a file. The printable characters defined by ASCII are 32 (a space) through 126 (a tilde: "~").

A true ASCII text file is one that contains a series of printable characters separated by a carriage return (ASCII value of 13) and a line feed character (ASCII value of 10). Each of these carriage return/line feed pairs denotes the end of a line and the beginning of another line.

ASCII text files are probably the most common file format used by your PC. Virtually every program that can read and write files can read and write ASCII text files. For example, the Notepad accessory, provided with Windows, can read and write ASCII text files just fine.

In addition, VBA provides statements and functions that make reading and writing ASCII text files line by line a breeze. Those statements are covered in detail later in this chapter.

Foreign File Formats

Many programs maintain information in their own special file formats. These formats are simply layouts that were created for use with the program because the program's developers decided it was best for them to store their data in that manner.

There are many examples of different types of data formats. For example, Excel stores its workbooks in .XLSX and .XLSM files and its templates in .XLTX and .XLTM files. Other programs—like Word, Access, and PowerPoint—store their files using different formats. The list could go on and on.

These file formats were originally designed by the developer(s) of the program. Some of these formats have been published so that anyone who wants to read and update them can do so. Other formats are considered trade secrets and the only way to figure them out (short of hiring a spy) is to spend a lot of time with a program that lets you look at each character in the file—although this is much like trying to learn French by picking up a book written in French and simply trying to read it. Some people can do it, but it takes a long time and a lot of perseverance!

Provided you know the format of a specific file, you can write routines in VBA to read, write, and update any foreign file type you want. This writing is done using the binary file processing capability of the language, which is covered later in this chapter.

Import/Export Formats

Although many programs maintain information in files of their own format, there are several common file interchange formats used for importing and exporting into and out of programs. These common formats are understood by many programs and facilitate the transfer of information from one program to the next.

Examples of these format types are the Comma-Separated Values (.CSV) format for transferring spreadsheet information from one program to another. Another example is an older format known as the Data Interchange Format (.DIF) which is used to transfer information from one spreadsheet program to another. There are many other special formats in use today, and there will be many more designed and used in the future.

Often these import/export file formats are simply specially formatted ASCII text files. These types of files can be easily viewed and edited with a text editor such as Notepad. Even so, these files contain additional information needed by programs during the import of the data.

VBA provides direct support for an import/export format often referred to as a *delimited text file.* Here's an example of what the contents of such a file might look like:

```
"Mike Schinkel",31,"Atlanta","GA"
"Michelle Brookshire",26,"Clermont","GA"
"Matt Adams",30,"Buford","GA"
"Traci Detchon",36,"Smyrna","GA"
```

Using either VBA's ASCII or binary file processing capability, you have the tools you need to process any type of import/export file that you may find.

File Basics

Because data files are external to your programs, you must take certain steps to allow your program to access the information contained in the files. Essentially, your macro must establish a line of communication with a file before it can process it. When you finish using a file, you should cut off that line of communication because each open line of communication requires resources to maintain.

Opening a File

In the same way you open the door of a filing cabinet before you can browse through its files, your VBA code must open a file before it can read or update its contents. The statement to do this is Open. Using only its most basic options, you can open files for reading (Input), writing (Output), or appending (Append).

The basic format for the Open statement is

```
Open filename [for mode] As filenum
```

You must use Open before attempting to read or write from the file. The *filename* parameter must be a valid filename. The optional *mode* specifier can be any of these: Input, Output, or Append. Finally, the *filenum* can be any integer value from 1 to 255. Here are some examples:

```
Open "c:\someplace\myfile.txt" For Input As 1
Open "errorlog.txt" For Append As 2
```

When you open a file you must specify a file number. This file number is subsequently used to refer to the line of communication between your macro and the file on disk. Whenever you need to read from, write to, or otherwise manipulate an open file, you need to use the file number you specified when you opened the file.

The mode that you specify when you open the file is important as well. If you open a file for Input, then you will only be able to read from the file. If you open it for Output, you will only be able to write to the file and VBA starts writing to the file at the beginning. (This presents the very real possibility of wiping out and overwriting an existing file.) If you instead specify Append, you can only write to the file, but VBA starts writing at the end if the file already exists. You learn how to both read and write to the same open file later in this chapter.

Handling File Errors

When you open a file, there is unfortunately a good chance that something could go wrong—for example, the file could be missing. Because of this fact, you must be sure to provide error handling for any routines that open files.

The easiest way for you to handle an error on the Open statement is to use On Error Resume Next and then check the Err function afterwards. The Err function returns a non-zero number identifying the error if an error did occur on the Open statement. The values returned by the Err function are listed in VBA's online help system.

The following example illustrates how to trap and identify file errors; you yourself have to determine what to do in case of an error, as the error handling required for each is likely to be different.

```
On Error Resume Next
Open "c:\myfile.txt" For Input As 3
If Err <> 0 Then
    MsgBox ("File Error: " + Str$(Err))
End If
```

Reading Data Files

After opening a file, the easiest way to read from it is to read the entire file. You can do this using a combination of the two functions: Input and Lof. The Input function reads data from a file and returns it as a string.

You should use the Input function with a file opened using the Input mode of the Open statement. You specify two parameters with the function: the number of bytes (characters) to read from the file and the file number you specified when you opened the file. Here's a simple example that reads 1,024 bytes from a file:

```
Dim sRawText As String

Open "c:\myfile.sys" For Input As 3
sRawText = Input(1024, 3)
```

The Lof function is used to figure out the length of a file. It returns the number of bytes in a file. For instance, this is how you would determine the length of a specific file on your system:

```
Dim lFileSize As Long

Open "c:\someplace\mybigfile.txt" For Input As 1
lFileSize = Lof(1)
```

You can use the Input function with the Lof function to retrieve an entire file into a string variable. This technique is one of the simplest ways of reading a file, but you won't want to read very large files in this manner. Here's the technique for reading the file:

```
Dim sFileText As String

Open "c:\myfile.txt" For Input As 5
sFileText= Input(Lof(5), 5)
```

Closing Files

Just as it is a good idea to close your file cabinet drawers after you are through with them (so you don't bang your shin!), you should also close your program's data files as soon as you no longer need to have them open. A simple Close statement is all that is required to release the line of communication between the program and the file.

You can use Close with or without a file number. If you use a file number, it should be the number of a file you previously opened. If you don't use a file number, then the statement closes any files you previously opened. Either of these is an acceptable use of Close:

```
Close
Close 2
```

It is a good idea for you to close a file as soon as possible to avoid potential problems. Because Windows does not always write information to the disk when you expect it to (it waits until an internal output buffer is full), you cannot be sure that what you sent to the file is actually written to it until you close the file. Because it is better to be safe than sorry, close the file as soon as you can.

Types of File Access

There are three file access modes you can use when working with files:

- Sequential-access
- Random-access
- Binary-access

As discussed earlier, each of these three methods of accessing files has its own particular purpose.

Sequential Files

A sequential file is one written and read from the beginning to the end, in order, much like how tape is played in a tape player. The typical tape player cannot skip to the next song on the tape; instead, it must play or fast-forward through the entire song.

So, a sequential file is one that you can only read in the order that it was written. The reason for this is there is no predetermined structure, and there are no clues for what data is located where.

Reading ASCII Text Files

A perfect example of a sequential file is an ASCII text file. A text editor such as Notepad reads an ASCII text file line by line into memory and then later writes the entire file back out to disk, typically overwriting the previous copy of the file.

In your VBA programs, you may want to read ASCII text files so you can modify them. For example, you may want to update your AUTOEXEC.BAT PATH statement. Or, you may want to write a utility to extract information like the names of subroutines and functions from the VBA code you may export to a disk file (see Chapter 5). Or, you can choose from a multitude of other tasks you can accomplish.

To read the data in an ASCII text file, you must first open the file for input and then use the Line Input # statement. Here is how you use the statement:

```
Dim sRawText As String

Open "myfile.txt" For Input As 3
Line Input #3, sRawText
```

You should note that the # mark is necessary in this statement. Without it, VBA generates an error. The Line Input # statement reads a line from the specified file into the string variable you supply.

As mentioned earlier, you can use the Line Input # statement to read a line in an ASCII text file, but ASCII text files often contain more than one line. Obviously, you may need to read more than one line so what do you do? Do you use two Line Input # statements to read two lines, three statements to read three lines, and so on? Of course not! You read lines inside a loop such as a While loop.

But that creates another problem—how do you know when you've reached the last line in the file? Easy. VBA provides an Eof (end-of-file) function that tells you when you have read the last line in the file (but not before).

As an example, assume that you have a file on your system that consists of individual lines of data. Some of the lines of data begin with the characters "CTL" and others begin with the characters "DET". You may want to pull all the lines beginning with "DET" and display them. Here's how you do it:

```
Sub DisplayDetail()
    Dim sTemp As String
    Dim sMessage As String

    On Error Resume Next
    Open "myfile.txt" For Input As 3
    If Err = 0 Then
        sMessage = ""
        Do Until Eof(3)
            Line Input #3, sTemp
            If Left(sTemp, 3) = "DET" Then
                sMessage = sMessage & Mid(sMessage, 4) & vbCrLf
            End If
        Loop
        Close 3
    Else
        sMessage = "Error opening file"
    End If
    MsgBox sMessage
End Sub
```

Writing to ASCII Text Files

Now that you have read ASCII text files in, you may want to learn how to write them out as well. You write ASCII text files out by using the Print # statement. There are two forms of the Print # statement, as shown here:

```
Print #2, "My text"
Print #2, "My text";
```

Note that the only difference between the two is the semicolon at the end. The difference is that without the semicolon, VBA considers the line "complete" and terminates it with a carriage return/line feed pair. If you don't want the line to be terminated, then include the semicolon.

Suppose you want to update the macro introduced in the previous section so that the detail information is extracted from one file and written out to another file.

```
Sub ExtractDetail()
    Dim sTemp As String
    Dim sMessage As String

    On Error Resume Next
    Open "myfile.txt" For Input As 3
    If Err = 0 Then
        Open "extractfile.txt" For Output As 4
        If Err = 0 Then
            sMessage = ""
            Do Until Eof(3)
                Line Input #3, sTemp
                If Left(sTemp, 3) = "DET" Then
                    Print #4, Mid(sMessage, 4)
                End If
            Loop
            Close
        Else
            sMessage = "Error opening output file"
        End If
    Else
        sMessage = "Error opening input file"
    End If
    MsgBox sMessage
End Sub
```

Reading Delimited Text Files

As stated earlier, a delimited text file is an ASCII file, but it is an ASCII file for which VBA provides some special processing capabilities. Often you may use these file formats to import from or export to database or spreadsheets programs.

To read delimited text files, you can use the Input # statement. The basic format for the statement is:

```
Input #filenum, var1 [, var2] [..., varN]
```

The Input # statement reads a line from the file identified by *filenum* and parses the information in the file into the variables *var1* through *varN* that you specify. For example:

```
Dim sFullName As String
Dim iAge As Integer
Dim sCity As String
Dim sState As String

Open "myfile.csv" For Input As #1
Input #1, sFullName, iAge, sCity, sState
```

When you use the Input# statement, you must be sure that the file you are reading and the variables you are using coincide in number and in type. If you do not specify enough variables to hold all the data to be read in or if you specify too few, VBA gets confused and you end up getting garbage in your variables.

Writing Delimited Text Files

The converse of the Input # statement is the Write # statement. This statement creates a file that can be read back into numerous other programs or into VBA using the Input # statement:

```
Dim sFullName As String
Dim iAge As Integer
Dim sCity As String
Dim sState As String

Open "myfile.csv" For Ouput As #3
Write #3, sFullName, iAge, sCity, sState
```

Random-Access Files

As compared to a sequential file, a random-access file is one that can be read and written in any order. You may want to think of a random-access file as being like a compact disc instead of a cassette tape. Just like a compact disc where you can select and play tracks in any order, you can read, write, and even update portions of a random-access file in any order.

Random-access files were originally provided to allow BASIC programmers an easy way to create databases. What is a database? A database is simply a collection of related information organized in a structured way. In earlier days, BASIC programmers created relatively sophisticated database applications using random-access files as the tables in a relational database. Today, however, you would probably not want to use random-access files to implement a complex database program. VBA provides much greater database capabilities via the powerful Access Database Engine. (How you do this is beyond the scope of this book.)

Random-access files are useful if you need to create a relatively simple database or if you need to read and update data that was created by a program that uses that format.

Record Variables: User-Defined Types

Processing random-access files means processing records. As such, you must define the records in your file, which is done by using the Type…End Type block statement. After you have defined your structure you can create variables using that definition and then store the values contained in these variables directly into the records of your random-access file.

This format for the Type…End Type statement is illustrated in this example:

```
Type GolfCart
    Model As String * 10
    Color As String * 15
    Seats As Integer
    Horses As Single
End Type
```

Use the Type…End Type statement to define the structure of a record in your random-access file. In this example a new data type called GolfCart is created.

The new data type must be added to the Declarations area of your modules. You do that by simply using the Procedure drop-down list in the upper-right corner of the Code window to specify the (Declarations) area, as shown in Figure 15-1.

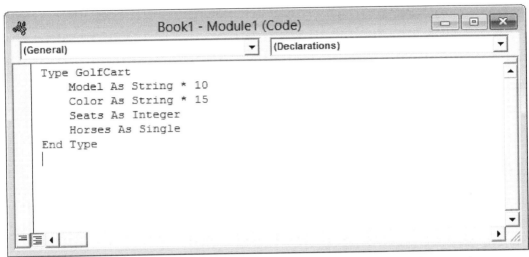

Figure 15-1. *Your user-defined data types must be added in the (Declarations) area.*

Once defined, you can then use the definition in your macro:

```
Dim MyCart As GolfCart

MyCart.Model = "Bogie XL"
MyCart.Color = "Fairway Green"
MyCart.Seats = 2
MyCart.Horses = 10
```

In this example a variable called MyCart is declared as using the GolfCart data type. Values are assigned to individual members of the MyCart variable by separating the variable name (MyCart) from the member names (Model, Color, Seats, and Horses) with a period. This method of addressing members is consistent with how VBA addresses other objects and members.

You must be aware of the size of the structure (in bytes) that you create using the Type...End Type statement. This awareness is important when you open the random-access file, as discussed in the next section. The easiest way to determine the length of your records is by using the Len function. For example you could determine the length of the MyCart variable using a single line of code:

```
iRecLen = Len(MyCart)
```

Opening Random-Access Files

To open a file for random-access, you should specify For Random in the Open statement instead of Input, Output, or Append. In addition, you should specify the record size in bytes using the Len= clause:

```
Open "myfile.dat" For Random As 3 Len = iRecLen
```

Reading Records from Random-access Files

When you have a file open for random access, you can read any record simply by using the Get statement. This statement reads a specific record number into the variable you indicate in this manner. For instance, the following example fetches the fifth record from the file and places its contents in the MyCart variable:

```
Get #3, 5, MyCart
```

If you use Get without a record number then it fetches the next record from the file:

```
Get #3, , MyCart
```

You can omit the record number in the Get statement if you want. The following example provides a simple illustration of reading records from a file sequentially using the Get statement.

```
Dim MyCart As GolfCart
Dim iRecLen As Integer
Dim lRecNum As Long
Dim J As Integer

iRecLen = Len(MyCart)
Open "myfile.dat" For Random As 3 Len = iRecLen
lRecNum = Lof(3) / iRecLen
```

```
Dim Carts(lRecNum) As GolfCart

For J = 1 to lRecNum
    Get #3, , Carts(J)
Next J
Close 3
```

Although you have seen how to read records sequentially using the Get statement, you can read them in any order. You only need be careful that you do not read a record that does not yet exist in the file; if you attempt to do so, VBA triggers an error.

Writing Records to Random-Access Files

The converse of the Get statement is the Put statement. It is used to write records to a random-access file. All you need to do is make sure you supply a record number and a variable that you want written:

```
Put #3, 5, MyCart
```

If you leave off the record number then Put writes the next record in the file:

```
Put #3, , MyCart
```

Binary Files

As compared to both sequential and random-access files which access files essentially at the record level, binary files are accessed byte by byte. As such, binary files have no limitations whatsoever; you can process a binary file any way you like (assuming that you designed the format of the file). On the other hand, nothing is done for you automatically with binary files; you must determine exactly where to place data into the file and then specify that information to VBA.

Actually, there is no such thing as a binary file; any file can be opened for binary access. You can read, write, and update information for every type of file ever created on a PC using binary mode, assuming that you know the file's format!

Opening Files for Binary Access

To open a file for binary access, you should specify For Binary on the Open statement. Because binary files are accessed byte by byte, you do not need to specify a Len clause as you did for random-access files:

```
Open "c:\someplace\MyCustomers.dat" For Binary As 5
```

Reading from Binary Access Files

When you have opened a file for binary access, you can use the Get statement to read information from the file into variables. You can also specify where in the file you want reading to start:

```
Get #5, 100, sTemp
```

In this case the Get statement reads the file starting with byte 100 and places the input into the sTemp string. You could also read from the current file location by leaving out the start specification:

```
Get #5, , sTemp
```

You need to make sure that sTemp is the length you want before you try to use Get; it is the length of the variable that determines how many bytes are read from the file. In other words, if you want to make sure that 25 bytes are read from the file, you just need to set the length of the variable before using Get:

```
sTemp = Space(25)
Get #5, 100, sTemp
```

Writing to Binary-Access Files

Writing to a binary file is as easy as reading; you simply use the Put statement to write information from a variable into the file:

```
Put #5, 100, sTemp
```

The Put statement writes the contents of sTemp to the file, starting at (in this case) byte 100. The length of sTemp determines how many bytes are written to the file. The starting position is optional and, if omitted, the Put statement writes to the file starting at the next byte in the file.

Updating the Current Position in a Binary File

If you use binary-access files you may need to move to a specific position in a file so you can begin accessing a portion of the file in a sequential manner. You can use the Seek statement to update the current file position. All you need to do is provide the file number and the position within the file:

```
Seek #3, 200
```

The Seek statement updates the current file pointer position for the file so that the next byte, read or written, is the byte you specified.

Determining the Current Position in a Binary File

As you start to work with binary files, you soon find out that there are two positions that are of importance: the last byte processed and the next byte to be processed. These positions are always offset from each other by one byte.

The last byte processed is determined with the Loc statement, in this manner:

```
Dim lFilePostion As Long
Dim lNextWrite As Long

lFilePosition = Loc(3)
```

If you had just written 150 bytes to the beginning of file 3, then after the above code lFilePosition would be equal to 150. You can find out where the next data will be written by using the Seek statement without a position specification, in this manner:

```
lNextWrite = Seek(3)
```

In this case lNextWrite would be equal to 151, which is where the next writing will occur. You can use Seek (or Loc) to save and later restore your positions in a binary file as shown here:

```
Dim iSavePos As Integer

Open "orders.dbf" For Binary As #3
iSavePos = Seek(3)        'Get current position
...                       'Do something here
Seek #3, iSavePos         'Return to previous position
```

16

Debugging and Error Handling

Debugging is the process of removing bugs. You wouldn't have to debug your programs if you just didn't put bugs into them in the first place. Unfortunately, programming is a process which is prone to errors. It is sometimes difficult for you to express your ideas with words and after all, words are a significant part of what you use to program computers.

In this chapter you learn how you can use the tools provided with VBA to debug your programs. You'll also learn some techniques that you can apply during the development process—techniques that can greatly diminish the potential for bugs creeping in your programs in the first place.

What Are Bugs?

If you look in a good programmer's dictionary, you discover that bugs are errors either in hardware or software that cause a computer operation to malfunction. That is not all, however. Bugs also can cause hardware or software to function differently than you would expect. The bottom line is that bugs can cause you hours and hours of headaches when you are programming.

Bugs of many different types can creep into your programming code. These typically fall into only a few categories, however:

- Syntax-related
- Logic-related
- Operation-related

Syntax-Related Errors

Just as grammar is important in ensuring what you say is understood by other people, *syntax* is vital in making VBA understand what you want done by the computer. Like your ever-watchful mother and father correcting your use of "ain't" and other grammatical mistakes, VBA flags you when it doesn't understand your use of its language. This flagging generally occurs when you attempt to run the program.

Correct syntax, however, doesn't guarantee a working program—at least not if "working" means that the program performs the intended task. Consider the following, grammatically correct, sentence.

```
The far off chickens meow as the blinding flash of darkness settles.
```

What? Chicken meow? Blinding darkness? This is nonsense. Yet, it complies with the grammatical requirements of English. In the same way, you can write syntactically correct programs for VBA that have the same chance of executing properly as the sentence above has of being understood.

Syntax errors are relatively easy to fix, particularly because VBA helpfully points out where the error occurred and gives you a bit of information to help understand what is happening.

Logic-Related Errors

Logic, in computers, typically means the process and order in which tasks are accomplished. For example, you may want to display information on-screen about the contents of a file. It appears that the records display properly, but for some reason, the subtotals don't come out right. Chances are good that this is a logic error—there is something wrong in the code that is causing the wrong figures to add up.

Logic errors can be the most tedious and troublesome errors to find and correct. This is because you typically have to take a "larger approach" view of your program, trying to figure out what happened where and why.

Operation-Related Errors

Operation-related errors are closely related to logic errors, but there are some subtle differences. Operation errors are the kind that generally result from surpassing the limits of the tools you are using. For example, suppose you have written a program and one of the following occurs:

- You exceed the storage capability of a variable.

- You attempt to do a division and the divisor is zero.

- You surpass the precision of a data type.

Each of these results in incorrect data being used, and the second one results in an error when it is encountered. These types of errors can be detected and compensated for, however, if you think through how your program is to be used.

Why are Bugs a Problem?

The manufacturer of a computer goes through several major steps to get the machine into your hands.

1. Design of the computer.

2. Placement of components upon circuit boards.

3. Attachment of circuit boards and other subsystems (power supply, disk drives, and so on) to the chassis and interconnection with other components.

4. Shipping to the vendor.

Whereupon you can purchase your computer.

At any step along the way a defect can be introduced that may render your new machine inoperable. If your computer isn't designed properly, it will never work. If the parts were plugged into the wrong locations on the circuit board, you'll need a new one. If the power supply wasn't wired to the circuit board properly, you'll probably need a whole new machine.

Suppose a part was misplaced in step 2. If there wasn't any testing along the way, all the other labor and material that goes into the computer is worthless. The machine won't work and the manufacturer incurs significant cost in replacing it.

But if the circuit board is tested immediately after part insertion (as they are), the mistake would be found and corrected at a time when the cost is minimal.

As a general rule of thumb, mistakes that go uncorrected cost ten times as much to fix at the next major processing step. If two steps are skipped before the mistake is caught then the cost is 100 times what it would have been had it been corrected immediately. This is why testing occurs at each major step of most manufacturing processes.

The time it takes you to fix a bug in your program works exactly the same way. If you have an error in your basic design you might have to redo the entire application. The time expense in this case is enormous. If you mistype something in a code module and have to track it down after the entire program is complete, it's not as bad as a design flaw. But it can still be time consuming, especially when you consider that most of these errors are avoidable.

So, before you learn about the techniques for removing bugs, it is only appropriate that you review some steps to help prevent them from occurring in the first place.

Keeping Bugs Out

You have already been introduced to several good practices for keeping bugs out of your programs in this book. Because they are so important, take a moment to review them and learn about a few new ones.

- **Use meaningful variable names.** When you are concentrating on programming, it is easy to forget what a variable named J or K2 is for. It takes much less effort to recall the purpose of a variable called iOuterLoopCounter or iMaxCharsPerLine. Every little bit helps and the less you need to concentrate on what a variable is used for, the more you can concentrate on how you are using it.

- **Declare all variables.** Explicit declaration prevents errors due to misspelling. It also guards against another error—data-type confusion. When a variable is undeclared, it most often assumes the type of Variant. Because Variants can hold almost anything, you won't get an error when you assign a string value to a Variant that you intended only to hold numbers or vice versa.

- **Keep procedures short.** Each Function and Sub procedure should perform one specific task—no more and no less. If you fit all the code in a procedure on-screen at once, it is easier to understand. Again, the fewer details, the more you can concentrate on the real task.

- **Test functionality as you go.** Like the manufacturing example given earlier in the chapter, much of your code serves as a basis for later programming stages. By testing each function and subroutine independently, you can isolate errors that, when fixed immediately (while the code is fresh in your mind), aren't terribly expensive to fix. If you don't find the error for a day or more, you may have forgotten how the code functions and you'll need to spend valuable time recalling its purpose. If the error isn't found until after other code has built upon that procedure, there is the chance that you not only need to modify the routine in which the error appears, but also those that use it. Catch and fix your mistakes as early as possible.

- **Verify your design before programming.** If your algorithms are faulty to begin with, no amount of programming can fix them. Even though you are probably anxious to implement your ideas and start coding immediately, resist this temptation. The number of errors that are tracked to faulty logic is surprising. This type of error is very costly to fix because often most of the program must be rewritten.

- **Add meaningful comments to your procedures.** Even if your program works correctly now, at some time in the future you may want to add features, or someone else may be charged with maintaining it. Code without useful comments is like a jigsaw puzzle—a challenge, at best. Commenting your code is like writing assembly instructions on the pieces of the puzzle—they make life much easier. It is good to comment the purpose of each procedure.

Usually a line or two at the beginning describing what values are expected, what the routine does, and what, if any, values are returned.

What is Debugging?

As you learned earlier in the chapter, debugging is the process of removing bugs from your program. How hard it is to get rid of errors depends on many things: the complexity of your program, the variability of your data, the design process you went through, and your temperament.

Many people say that debugging is actually an art. There is an element of truth in this, because programming is also an art. Some people can sit down in front of a computer, look at code, and immediately comprehend what is wrong. Others can labor for hours, staring at the same code over and over before getting a glimpse of what the problem is.

A programmer is also, by nature, a debugger—you have to be. After all, you understand your programming code more intimately than anyone else. You are not left to fend for yourself, however. VBA provides a series of tools that you can use to debug your macros. The balance of this chapter helps you understand what those tools are and how you can use them in your debugging efforts.

Getting Rid of Bugs

Even if you exercise all the precautions mentioned earlier in this chapter, it always seems that somehow bugs still manage to get through the cracks. This has nothing to do with experience or effort; it simply seems to be a fact of life. Thus, you need to learn how to use the VBA debugging tools—it is inevitable.

When it comes to debugging, the best teacher is experience. In that vein, you should "learn by doing." With that in mind, let's try a short little program that puts information into an Excel worksheet. Open a new workbook (you should only have the one workbook open) and then press ALT+F11. This displays the Visual Basic Editor. Make sure you have a single procedure, like this:

```
Sub TestingMacro()
    Dim MyVar1 As String
    Dim MyVar2 As String
    Dim MyVar3 As String

' The following is the first portion of the test
    MyVar1 = 5
    MyVar2 = 7
    Range("A1").Value = MyVar1 + MyVar2

' The following is the second portion of the test
    For J = 10 To 1
        MyVar3 = "A" & J+2
        Range(MyVar3).Value = J
    Next J
End Sub
```

Don't be alarmed if, as you are entering this code, you see bugs right away—they are supposed to be there. You learn how to use the VBA tools to uncover and remove these bugs.

The first portion of the test is supposed to add the numbers stored in MyVar1 and MyVar2 and then insert them into cell A1. The second portion of the test is supposed to count down from 10 to 1, putting each number into a different cell in column A.

Now run the TestingMacro and take a look at what you see in the worksheet. What's this? You immediately notice that the program gives the wrong result:

	A	B
1	57	
2		
3		
4		
5		

You are trying to add the numbers 5 and 7, which should result in 12, but you get 57 instead. Something is very wrong; there must be a problem with the logic. In addition, the numbers 10 through 1 should appear lower in column A, but they don't. There must be something wrong here, as well.

You could try to analyze the code you've written to determine what is wrong, but that may not be fruitful since you wrote the code in the first place and it obviously isn't working. Let's see what the Visual Basic Editor has in its bag of debugging tricks to help out. After you have a few more tools to work with, you can attack the bugs in this project.

Single Stepping

One of the primary reasons computers are such powerful tools is that they can execute thousands of instructions each second. This ability gives them the blindingly fast speed necessary for calculating thousands of spreadsheet cells in a second, a task that would take you hours, or perhaps days.

If your program isn't behaving the way you expected, this speed can present a problem. How do you isolate a bug to a particular area of your program if thousands of lines are zinging by every second? There is no way for you to see what is happening.

Single stepping is part of the solution to this problem. As its name implies, single stepping lets you step through your program one line at a time. To single step, in the Visual Basic Editor make sure the insertion point is somewhere within the TestingMacro procedure. Then, select Single Step from the Debug menu or press **F8**. The first line of code in your program is executed and the program pauses, awaiting your next command. Press the **F8** key again and the next line of your code is executed. You can tell which line is ready to be executed because it appears in yellow. You should press the **F8** key a total of four times; your screen will appear as shown in Figure 16-1.

After each press of **F8** your program is paused. When paused, the program is neither terminated nor running. It isn't executing, but it hasn't been unloaded from memory. One of the most advantageous things you can do when a VBA program is paused is examine memory variables.

What's Its Value?

When a program is paused (you are single stepping through it), you can examine the value of variables contained in the current procedure. Variables

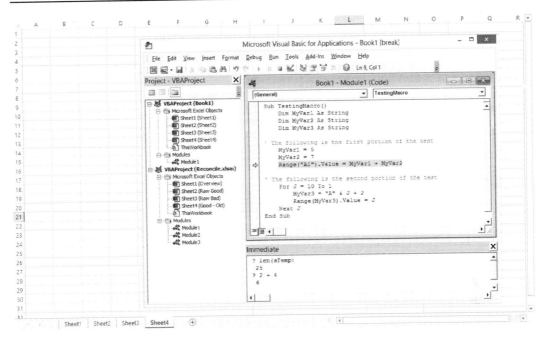

Figure 16-1. *Single stepping through your program.*

in other procedures are not visible unless they have been declared as Global variables (see Chapter 2).

You should already be single stepping through your program, as described in the previous section. You've executed the first two lines of your program, where the values of MyVar1 and MyVar2 are set. Your program is now waiting for you to do something.

The line that is highlighted in the Code window is the next line that will be executed. Remember the problem from when you first ran the program? The number 57 appeared in cell A1 instead of the number 12, as it should have. Let's look at the variables and see if we can determine why.

Hover the mouse pointer over the variable name MyVar1 in the highlighted line. After a short time you should see a ToolTip appear, telling you the value of MyVar1 ("MyVar1 = 5"). You can also hover the mouse pointer over MyVar2 and see its value.

Now, using your mouse select the words *MyVar1 + MyVar2* in the Code window. Choose Debug | Quick Watch or press **SHIFT+F9**. You see a small Quick

Watch window displayed, as shown in Figure 16-2. This window contains the expression you are evaluating (in the Expression box) and its current value (in the Value box).

The value of the expression in the Quick Watch window shows that the two values are concatenated; they are not added as expected. Apparently there is something wrong with the formula, even though the individual variables in the formula are correct. Ahh! You have narrowed your problem down to a logic error in your formula.

Because there is only one operator in this formula (the plus sign), it is easy to find the problem. The next step is to look in the on-line help to discover how the plus operator is supposed to work. Press **F1** to display the help system and

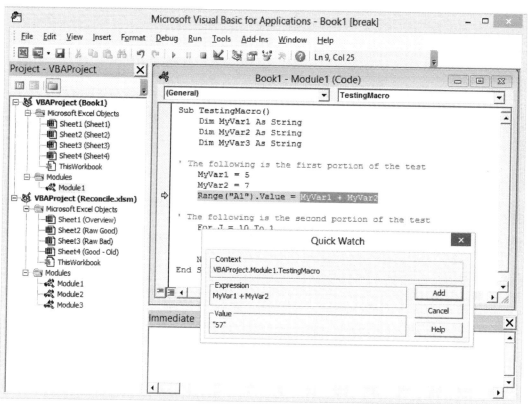

Figure 16-2. *A Quick Watch window shows you the value of an expression.*

after a bit of poking around you can discover that if the operands (MyVar1 and MyVar2) are strings, the plus sign concatenates them. The problem your program is exhibiting is that it is interpreting the numbers you have entered as strings and therefore isn't adding them. (This makes sense since you defined the variables as strings in the program.)

To fix this problem and make the plus sign work like you want it to, you must be using numeric values. The way to do this is change the variable declarations so that they are using a numeric data type. To make this change, follow these steps:

1. Stop your program (remember, it is still paused) by clicking Run | Reset.

2. Change the first two lines of the program so they look like this:

    ```
    Dim MyVar1 As Integer
    Dim MyVar2 As Integer
    ```

Now you can run the program and verify that what you see in the worksheet is correct:

The output from the first portion of the test is now correct, but there is still no output from the second portion of the test.

Stepping By Procedures

So far you have learned how to single step through your program and examine variables, an immense aid in determining where something has gone wrong.

You can figure out (by hand, if necessary) what value a variable should contain at a certain point in the program and you can compare that with the value it actually contains. If the two are different, you can backtrack and determine where things went wrong.

While you are single stepping through a procedure, you may come across a program line that calls another procedure. If you continue single stepping by pressing **F8** you see the code for that procedure and single step through it as well. If you are confident the error does not lie in the procedure, you may not want to do this. You want to skip that procedure, instead of executing right through it. VBA allows you to do this by using a *procedure step*.

Procedure steps execute procedures at full speed. They don't skip the procedure; they just run it at its normal speed, which usually results in an immediate return. To step by (or *step over*) a procedure, use **SHIFT+F8**. If the next line of code is not a procedure call, the procedure step button behaves as a single step.

Breakpoints

Stepping through your program a line at a time can quickly become tedious—particularly if you have to step through large amounts of code that have already been tested. Even stepping a procedure at a time can be time consuming in a large macro. Isn't there a way to get right to the source of the suspected problem? Yes! This is why VBA allows you to set breakpoints.

A *breakpoint* is a setting you assign to a line of code that pauses the execution of your program when the line is encountered. A breakpoint is different from an End statement. End terminates the execution of your program and removes it from memory. A breakpoint temporarily pauses your program, allowing you to probe memory and then continue on from the point at which you broke execution.

Breakpoints are a convenience; they allow you to execute your program up to a certain point at full speed. You can then examine the value of variables and step a line, or a procedure, at a time to observe your program's behavior.

Setting a Breakpoint

Setting a breakpoint is easy. While your program is stopped or paused, just position the cursor on the line at which you want VBA to stop. Now click Debug | Toggle Breakpoint or press **F9**. That line appears highlighted in red, meaning that the breakpoint has been set.

When you later run the program and VBA encounters the line at which you have set a breakpoint, it does three things:

- Pause the program
- Display the Code window containing the procedure with the breakpoint
- Wait for your command

At this point, you can apply any other debugging tool you want so you can determine where the error lies.

You should note that when VBA pauses due to encountering a breakpoint, it doesn't execute the line at which it stops. That line is the next line to be executed.

Debugging Using Breakpoints

If you use a breakpoint in conjunction with single stepping, you can see why the second part of the test isn't working properly. Set a breakpoint on the first executable line in the second portion; it is the line on which the For loop starts.

Now run your program. VBA shows the Code window containing the breakpoint, as shown in Figure 16-3.

Now use the single step tool (**F8**) to start through the procedure. The first thing you notice is that VBA stepped right over the For loop in your code. How could that have happened? If you examine the first line closely, applying the information you learned in Chapter 7, you see that the J counter (used in the

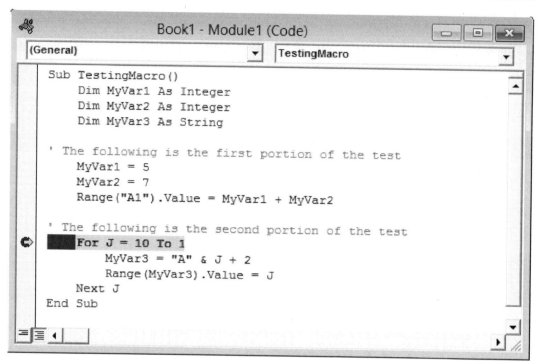

Figure 16-3. VBA stops when it reaches a breakpoint in your code.

For loop) starts with the value 10 and that the next value in the loop is 11. What you had intended, however, was for the loop to count backwards, from 10 to 1.

Aha! The problem seems to be that you forgot the Step -1 portion of the For loop, which would have made that happen. Add Step -1 to the end of the first statement in the loop, and it works as expected. You can single step through to see that each value is inserted in the worksheet:

	A	B	C
1	12		
2			
3	1		
4	2		
5	3		
6	4		
7	5		
8	6		
9	7		
10	8		
11	9		
12	10		
13			

The next step is to run the program at full speed to make sure it works properly. Before you can do this, however, you must remove the breakpoint. If you don't, then VBA dutifully stops each time it comes to the beginning of the second portion of the test.

To remove a breakpoint, stop your program and position the cursor on the line that contains the breakpoint. Then, click Debug | Toggle Breakpoint or again press **F9**. When you do, the breakpoint (and the tell-tale highlight) is removed.

After the breakpoints are removed, you can run your program at full speed. The output in the worksheet should look just as you expected at the beginning.

Watch Expressions

Earlier you learned how you can use the Quick Watch window to examine the contents of a variable or the results of an expression while your program is running. What if you want to watch the value over the course of the entire program, however? Continually selecting the Quick Watch tool could get very tedious. Fortunately, VBA allows you to set watches to help with this need.

Setting a watch, which in many ways is similar to setting a breakpoint, allows you to monitor the value of any variable in your program. Both the variable name and its value are continually shown in the Watch window. To set a watch expression, select the variable to watch by highlighting it. Then click Debug | Add Watch. You then see the Add Watch dialog box, shown in Figure 16-4.

The Add Watch dialog box allows you to modify exactly what VBA does while it watches the variable. If you only want to continually monitor the value of the variable, you can simply click the OK button. The variable you selected has now been added to the list of watch values. You can add more if you want.

If you run your program, the name of the variable appears in the Watch window. (You display the Watch window in the Visual Basic Editor by clicking View | Watch Window.)

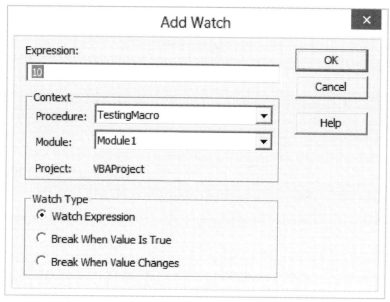

Figure 16-4. *VBA allows you to set watches that monitor variables and expressions for you.*

Breaking on Watches

If you set a breakpoint inside the loop, your program breaks each time the breakpoint is encountered. By using watches, however, you can cause VBA to break the loop only when the loop counter has reached a particular value. This approach is much more efficient when debugging. To see how it works, stop your program and follow these steps:

1. In the Code window, highlight the J variable in the start of the For loop.

2. Choose Debug | Add Watch. The Add Watch dialog box appears, as shown earlier in Figure 15-4.

3. In the Expression text box, enter a formula that defines when you want the program stopped. For example, you can enter the formula J = 4.

4. In the Watch Type box at the bottom of the dialog box, select the Break When Expression Is True option.

5. Click OK.

The watch has now been added. If you run your program you'll find that VBA pauses and enters Debug mode when the loop is encountered and J reaches 4.

Editing a Watch

As you are debugging your programs, it is not unusual to set a watch expression and then later need to change it. For example, you may decide that you want your macro to break when a particular variable contains the value 125 instead of 80. To edit a watch, just select the Edit Watch option from the Debug menu. You then see a list of watch expressions that have been set in your program. You can select any of the watches and click Edit to make your desired changes.

17

Resources

As I noted in the Introduction, this book is designed as an introductory book for working with macros. I wrote *Microsoft Excel VBA Guidebook* because I couldn't find a good entry-level guide anywhere. There are, however, lots of comprehensive references available for working with Excel macros.

Thus the reason for the resources listed in this chapter. Here I've listed only those books that I feel offer something unique in the macro-learning arena; you'll find my reasoning with each suggestion. The books are listed in a roughly alphabetic order and there are only ten of them. (They aren't listed in a "top ten" order, either.)

I've also included a QR code for each of the recommendations. If you have a phone or tablet that can use these nifty little codes, you'll be taken—in most instances—directly to a page on Amazon where you can learn more about the book and, if you want, order it. (Amazon Prime is a wonderfully addicting service.)

Happy learning!

ExcelTips: The Macros, Seventh Edition (Allen Wyatt, 2013). Sharon Parq Associates, Inc., 889 pgs., $41.99, 978-1-61359-201-4. An astonishing resource that allows you to develop your macro-writing skills through the use of hands-on examples and lucid explanations. I'm not biased at all, but I did write the book. ;-) You can even get a download version of this book for $7 less (only $34.99). The QR code takes you to the Tips.Net Store.

Excel 2010 Power Programming with VBA (John Walkenbach, 2010). Wiley, 1080 pgs., $49.99, 978-0-4704-7535-5. I've had a general rule about programming books for years: If it is authored by John Walkenbach, buy it. (Really; his stuff is that good.) John includes great examples and functions that illustrate more advanced VBA programming techniques.

Excel 2013 Power Programming with VBA (John Walkenbach, 2013). Wiley, 1104 pgs., $49.99, 978-1-118-49039-6. Updated for the latest version of Excel, this is a Walkenbach classic. It provides great depth and breadth of information that is at home on any reference shelf.

Mastering VBA for Microsoft Office 2010 (Richard Mansfield, 2010). Sybex, 912 pgs., $49.99, 978-0-470-63400-4. A hefty addition to any reference library, this book is especially valuable if you plan on creating VBA programs that work with more than just Excel.

Mastering VBA for Microsoft Office 2013 (Richard Mansfield, 2013). Sybex, 960 pgs., $49.99, 978-1-118-69512-8. Bigger and better than the previous edition that covered Office 2010. Includes more examples and nuggets you can put to use. I especially found the information on programming the ribbon to be helpful.

Microsoft Excel 2010 Programming by Example with VBA, XML, and ASP (Julitta Korol, 2011). Mercury Learning and Information, 1118 pgs., $49.95, 978-1-936420-03-2. Written as a series of example exercises, this book is a goldmine of great information. The section on programming Excel special features (Part 8, five chapters) is worth the price of the book alone. Includes a CD-ROM that has all the code examples from the book.

Professional Excel Development: The Definitive Guide to Developing Applications Using Microsoft Excel, VBA, and .NET (Rob Bovey, Dennis Wallentin, Stephen Bullen, and John Green, 2009). Addison-Wesley, 1176 pgs., $64.99, 978-0-

321-50879-9. This is the second edition of a book that deserves a place on any VBA programmer's shelf. It takes a highly structured approach to VBA development and helps readers understand the value in such an approach. Includes a CD-ROM with sample code from the book.

VBA and Macros: Microsoft Excel 2010 (Bill Jelen and Tracy Syrstad, 2010). Que, 656 pgs., $39.99, 978-0-7897-4314-5. Provides some great information on how to work with some advanced features of VBA. I especially found helpful the information on how to work with the newer data visualization tools from within your macros.

VBA and Macros: Microsoft Excel 2013 (Bill Jelen and Tracy Syrstad, 2013). Que, 648 pgs., $39.99, 978-0-7897-4861-4. Essentially a new edition of the earlier Excel 2010 version, updated specifically for Excel 2013. There are a few new nuggets in here, but if you already have the previous edition, you can probably safely skip this one. (Conversely, if you don't have the previous edition, then you will want to get this latest one.)

Writing Excel Macros with VBA, Second Edition (Steven Roman, 2002). O'Reilly, 576 pgs., $39.99, 978-0-596-00359-3. This is, by far, the oldest book to be included in this resource guide. There is a reason I've included it, though—it is very readable and provides great background information on how to program in VBA. This has, over the years, been a consistent "go to" book for me.

Index

Delimiter parameter, 210
Developer tab, displaying, 2–5
dialog boxes, 145–159
    Add Watch dialog box, 270
    built-in, 156–159
    Excel Options dialog box, 92–93
    Macro dialog box, 13, 55–56
    message boxes, creating, 146–153
    Modify Button dialog box, 93–94
    Options dialog box, 86–87
    PasteSpecial dialog box, 202–203
    Project Properties dialog box, 87–88
    Record Macro dialog box, 54–55
    References dialog box, 88–89
    user input, getting, 153–156
.DIF (Data Interchange Format), 240
Dim keyword, 31
Dim statement, 138–139
"disable all macros except digitally signed macros" setting, 7
"disable all macros with notification" setting, 7
"disable all macros without notification" setting, 7
DisplayAlerts property, 195
division
    integer and normal, 33
    modulus operator (Mod), 33–34
division operator, 33
Docking tab, 87
Do loop, 132–134
    exiting, 134
    first time through, 133
Double data type, 30

– E –

Editable parameter, 210
editing macros, 12–14
Editor Format tab, 87
Editor tab, 86
elements of macros, 19–50
    comments, adding, 26–27
    lines, continuing, 27–29
    operators, 32–38
    procedures, understanding, 21–26
    projects and modules, 20–21
    variables, 29–32

Else clause, 127
ElseIf statement, 123–124
Else statement, 123–124
"enable all macros" setting, 7
EnableEvents property, 58
"enable macros" notice, getting rid of, 14–17
enabling macros, 5–7
End statement, 266
EntireColumn property, 166, 200, 201
EntireRow property, 200, 201
enum. *See* enumerations
enumerations, 49–50, 52
Eof (end-of-file) function, 245
equal operator, 35
Eqv operator, 37
Erase, 140
Err function, 242
error handling. *See* debugging
event handlers, 57–67
    automatic macros, 68–69
    avoiding problems, 57–58
    and charts, 66–67
    and workbooks, 58–63
    and worksheets, 64–66
Excel Options dialog box, 92–93
exclamation mark icon, 150
execution, conditional. *See* conditional execution
Exit Do statement, 134
Exit For statement, 134
explicit formatting, 173–174
exponentiation operator, 33
exporting macros, 97–99

– F –

feedback, user, 152–153
file access, types, 244–253
    binary files, 251–253
    random-access files, 248–251
    sequential files, 244–247
file extensions, 54–55
FileFormat parameter, 216

Made in the USA
San Bernardino, CA
08 October 2017